setting
Sharyn Craig
solutions

C&T PUBLISHING

© Sharyn Craig 2001
Editor: Beate Marie Nellemann
Technical Editor: Karyn Hoyt
Copy Editor: Steve Cook
Cover Design: Christina Jarumay
Book Design and Illustrations: Rose Shiefer © C & T Publishing 2001
Design Direction: Diane Pedersen
Production Assistants: Claudia Böhm and Stacy Chamness
Photography: Carina Woolrich
Front Cover: *Sister's Star*
Back Cover: *Starring the Blues*

Attention Teachers:
C & T Publishing, Inc. encourages you to use this book as a text for teaching. Contact us at 800-284-1114 or www.ctpub.com for more information about C & T Teachers Program.

We take great care to ensure that the information included in this book is accurate and presented in good faith, but no warranty is provided nor results guaranteed. Since we have no control over the choice of materials or products used, neither the authors nor C & T Publishing, Inc. shall have any liability to any person or entity with respect to any loss or damage caused directly or indirectly by the information contained in this book.

Library of Congress Cataloging-in-Publication Data

Craig, Sharyn Squier
Setting Solutions / Sharyn Craig.
   p. cm.
Includes bibliographical references and index.
   ISBN 1-57120-117-3
   1. Patchwork. 2. Quilting. I. Title.
   TT835 .C73322 2001
   746.46—dc21   00-010270

Trademarked (™) and Registered Trademarked (®) names are used throughout this book. Rather than use the symbol with every occurrence of a trademark and registered trademark name, we have only used the symbol the first time the product appears. We are using the names only in an editorial fashion and to the benefit of the owner, with no intention of infringement.

Published by C & T Publishing, Inc.
P.O. Box 1456
Lafayette, California 94549

Printed in Hong Kong
10 9 8 7 6 8 5 3 2 1

Table of Contents

Dedication

Writing a book is a long and involved process. Writing a book like this takes not only hours on the computer, but hours in the sewing room, in classes, and in workshops, not to mention the endless conversations with quilters about what their personal problems in quiltmaking include. Every minute I spend working on a project like this, is time away from my family and friends. I cannot tell you how blessed and grateful I am that these people not only understand but support my mission. I would also be quite remiss if I didn't mention a very special friend, Christiane Meunier of Chitra Publications, who sat in my sewing room in 1988 and said, "What book do you want to write? I want to publish it." Without her faith and encouragement and support I would never have written my first book, let alone this, my eleventh book. Thank you to my family, my friends, and my students. This book is dedicated and belongs to you.

Acknowledgements

There are so many quilters who should be individually named and thanked for their willingness to work on this book project with me. Space will not permit all the individuals who made blocks for various block-of-the-month projects, but hopefully they will recognize their blocks and share the pride that comes from knowing that without their block the quilt wouldn't have turned out the way it did. I do want to thank the following people (in no particular order) who each, in her own way, went an extra mile of the journey with me: Linda Packer, Laurine Leeke, Carolyn Smith, Ruth Gordy, Joanie Keith, Margret Reap, Harriet Love, Carole Shumaik, Nancy Nichols, Louise Hixon, Arlene Stamper, Linda Hamby, Mary Jo Manzuk, Barbara Hutchins, Marilyn Henderson, Lynn Kough, and Sally Collins. I would also like to acknowledge Sally Schneider who took personal time out of her very busy schedule to mentor me, and help me to be able to focus my ideas and thoughts on this subject. Her insight and experience as an author and editor is invaluable.

Thanks too to Moda, Fasco, and P & B fabrics for providing fabric for many of the quilts in this book. A special thank you to Hobbs Batting for the generous gift of batting that went into most of my quilts.

Thank you to my very first quilting teacher, Bobbie Winkleman, who encouraged me to figure it out for myself. If she had given me patterns for each quilt and told me that was what it had to look like, I probably would have believed her. Instead she provided the tools, but then let me use them any way I wanted. I hope that through the pages in this book I am able to pass that same gift along. My wish is that you all are able to pick up the tools and techniques I share, but then venture off on your own to find your own solutions.

Getting Set

Okay, it is time to get started. You are reading this book because you recognize that you need help. The title, *Setting Solutions*, promises you hope. You are anxious to find some answers to assist you in getting your blocks into a finished quilt top. Well, you are in the right place. With this book you will take a visual journey of quilts a number of different quilters have made using the problem-solving techniques presented here. Although there are no yardage requirements or exact instructions for creating these quilts, you will be able to see how the quilters dealt with the problems they encountered. You can then use the information for the blocks you have already lying around.

Starting on page 80, you will find a chapter of Project Maps for some of the quilts. They are like a blueprint to the soul of the quilt. I have selected several quilts for this chapter. I have tried to select quilts that are easy to construct, but for which the piecing structure is not necessarily easy to see by looking at the photograph of the finished quilt. I have deliberately presented these maps without the Focus block of the original quilt. You should then be able to see how you might insert your own Focus blocks into these same spaces. It is my hope that you can use my book as a reference guide, not a recipe book.

We are all very good at starting projects. It is fun to take a workshop and learn how to do a new technique. It is fun to pull fabric for a quilt you see in a book or magazine and make the blocks. But then what? Time has elapsed and the momentum has waned. You now have all these blocks lying around and the guilt sets in. I want to help you get over those feelings. I want to teach you to make quilts using blocks that already exist.

There are many reasons that keep quilters from finishing their blocks into quilt tops. Do you know why you haven't made a quilt from certain blocks? Let us try to find out what the roadblocks to completion might be.

STEP One

IDENTIFY THE PROBLEM

Why aren't the blocks in a quilt top already? What is stopping you? Why the frustration? Why do you have stacks of blocks and no finished tops?

The problem could be lack of motivation, but, because you have turned to this book for help, I don't think that is the main issue. If it was lack of motivation that kept the blocks from getting into a quilt, you would be very content to store them as blocks forever. So, there must be something else.

Size differential

What about size differential? Are your blocks different sizes? This is a very real problem for a lot of quilters. When the blocks are different sizes it is difficult to get them together into one quilt.

Color

What about color? Do you feel color challenged? Do you have a stack of blocks that feel "flat?" Did you make blocks from fabrics you loved, but somehow they "missed?" Perhaps you received the blocks from other people, maybe through a guild exchange. I bet there are a few of those blocks that you are less than charmed by.

Odd or strange number of blocks

Do you have an odd or strange number of blocks to work with? What is an odd number of blocks and how does this happen? Fourteen, for example, is an odd number of blocks to set together into one quilt. You might have an odd number of blocks because they came from a guild block-of-the-month. It also happens when you have nine blocks from a workshop, maybe four blocks left over from another project, and one block that was just an experiment. It does happen. But what do you do with fourteen blocks? What do you do with all these workshop starts, or leftover blocks from another quilt? All through this book you will see examples of quilts created with orphans and odd numbers. Watch for them, and study them to see how this problem is addressed.

Tired of the traditional settings

Perhaps you are just tired of the traditional settings and you are looking for something different. Are you bored with being safe? Could it be that you would like to make a quilt that is "special", because it is a one-of-a-kind? Are you looking for a more innovative way to set your blocks?

Before you can do anything with your blocks you must identify the problem. It might be one of the reasons I have just listed, or it could be something totally different.

STEP Two

ACKNOWLEDGE THE GOAL

What are your expectations? What would you like to accomplish? Put your goal into words.

Some examples of goals that I might use include:

- I want to fix the size differences.
- I want to make a pastel quilt for my guest room bed.
- I want some new quilts to decorate the house for Christmas.
- I want to make a quilt for my spouse's office.
- I want to do something less expected with my blocks.
- I just want to get these blocks out of the closet and into a quilt.

Specific goals, such as making a quilt for your daughter's graduation, are easier to force yourself to stick to. If your goal is "non-specific", like getting blocks out of the closet and into a quilt, then maybe it would be helpful to start by making up a reason to make this quilt. Most people find it easier to work on a quilt when it is

for something specific. How about making a baby quilt? Is anyone you know having a baby? Perhaps you could make a lap quilt for an elderly aunt in a nursing home. Could your blocks be turned into a cuddle quilt for some charitable organization? There is nothing like a deadline to get someone motivated.

Define what it is you hope to accomplish. Once you have stated it, then you can move on to the next step.

STEP Three

DEVELOP A PLAN

Once you know what your goal is, you can begin to analyze the possibilities for implementing it. If your goal is a quilt for your spouse's office, then think of the colors you need to work with. Think of the space where the quilt will be hanging, which will determine the approximate size you would make.

An important part of the plan is creating a deadline. If you have a due date you will be motivated to get your quilt together.

STEP Four

DEFINE THE RESOURCES

Now we stop thinking in the abstract and actually get down to the nitty-gritty. You have to get all the various blocks out of their hiding places and see what you have.

I know that some of you are very organized and have all your various blocks and projects in bags or boxes, all neatly labeled. But when did you last open that box to look at the blocks? Do you know exactly how many you have? Is there extra fabric that goes with the blocks? I also know that there are a lot of you that have no idea how many UFO's are lurking behind closed doors. Spending some time now evaluating and organizing your stash could be time well spent in the long run.

Make a list if it helps you to remember better. You might want to sort your blocks by color, size, or theme. These are your resources. These are the raw materials that you are going to be playing with.

When you have looked through everything, you need to settle on the blocks you want to work with first.

Anything you found that you think you might be able to use with these blocks needs to be in this pile. Go through your fabric and pull anything that you think might work—the bigger the pile, the better.

Once you have done this, you are ready to read on. We are going to start by tackling the problems one at a time. We will look at different ways to reconcile size differences in your blocks, and play with color in lots of different ways. You will see some innovative setting ideas to start your creative juices flowing. What I will **not** give you is rules. There will be no rules and no patterns. You have blocks. That is why you're here. You do not need to start from scratch to make more blocks to make a quilt. You just need to learn how to get the blocks you already have into a quilt.

Inspiration is much of what this book is about. Inspiration through a visual journey aimed at giving you some ideas and solutions. Many of the quilts in this book share a very common setting, but they look quite different. I am hoping to teach you how you can learn to make a quilt on your own through these quilts.

Oh, one more thing. Throughout this book you will see a lot of quilts made from blocks, which are the direct result of block exchanges. Some of the blocks came from guild block-of-the-month participation, and some from friendship groups. Perhaps you might have a group of quilter friends that would be interested in participating in a swap, especially now that you know there are successful ways to solve any of the problems that these blocks could present. I am also going to be listing all quilts that share the same blocks, and all quilts that share the same setting, so you can cross-reference various quilts and see how the same blocks or the same set can look totally different. So, with all this in mind, let the game begin.

Saturday Night Live, 1995, 44" x 64"
Sharyn Craig, quilted by Diane Beaubien

These blocks were leftover from an opportunity quilt I made in 1985. No two blocks were the same size. I didn't like the colors or fabrics used in the blocks. In this book you'll learn how to reconcile challenges like these and others, resulting in quilts that make you happy and proud!

CHAPTER ONE

Defining the Norm

In this chapter I will present, define, and talk about some of the terms that will be used throughout this book. There are many other terms associated with setting your blocks, but I have chosen to list only the ones that I work with, which are specific to the material found in these pages.

Flannel Design Wall

This is a rigid base covered with flannel or cotton batting to create a surface your blocks will adhere to during the design phase of making a quilt. You can make your own design wall with a flat flannel sheet, cotton batting, or cotton outing flannel purchased by the yard. You can make a simple flannel wall by thumb-tacking the flannel directly to the wall, or you can get much fancier by covering a piece of foam-core board (or any other sturdy board) with the flannel. You can mount the covered board to an existing wall, or merely lean it against a wall or piece of furniture. The larger the flannel design wall is, the better, but the size will obviously be governed by the size of your space and, ultimately, the size of the quilts you will be making.

Audition

Think of this term in the same way you would an actor trying out for a role in a movie. To audition a fabric is to let it try out with the blocks. We audition for color, pattern, and layout.

Focus block

Straight

Diagonal

Set

When the word "Set" is used as a noun, it refers to the way the blocks are arranged to create the finished quilt top. As a verb, it means the action of sewing the pieces together into the top.

Focus Blocks

These are the patterned blocks that you are primarily working with. Focus blocks can be appliquéd or pieced.

Straight or Diagonal

You can position your Focus blocks either straight or diagonally. Position straight set blocks so that the edges of the block are parallel to the edges of the quilt. Rotate blocks 90 degrees so that the corners point towards the edges of your quilt and they are diagonal. Another term used frequently that means the same thing as diagonal is "on point".

Tangent blocks

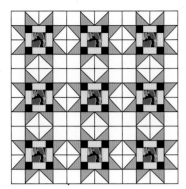

Straight

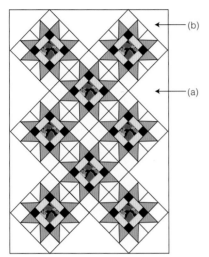

Diagonal

(a) Side Setting triangle
(b) Corner Setting triangle

When working with decimals and fractions, you will find it helpful to round up to the nearest ⅛''. If you would like your blocks to appear to float (not touch the edge), you can add an additional ½'' to 1'' to the amount you cut the squares. It's always better to be too big than too small. Refer to the Decimal Equivalent Chart on page 12 for assistance with these calculations.

Tangent Blocks

Tangent blocks are positioned next to one another. This set is sometimes referred to as "side by side." A tangent set can be either straight or diagonal.

Setting Triangles

When you position blocks on point, you will need to fill the outer edges of the quilt in with triangles. Triangles along the side of the quilt are called Side Setting. Corner Triangles fit the corners of the quilt. There are normally four Corner triangles, but the number of Side Setting triangles will vary, depending on the number of blocks in your quilt.

● **NOTE:** To calculate the size to cut the Side Setting triangles, you begin with the finished size of your block and multiply by 1.414. Add 1¼'' to that number. Cut a square equal to the sum and cut it twice, corner to corner. Cutting triangles this way will position straight of grain along the outer edge of the quilt, which is where you want the straight of grain in order to give your quilt top the most stability.

Example: 6'' blocks   6'' x 1.414 = 8.48 (or 8½'')

$8\frac{1}{2}'' + 1\frac{1}{4}'' = 9\frac{3}{4}''$

Cut a square 9¾'', cut twice

Each square yields four Side Setting triangles

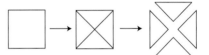

9¾'' square. Cut twice corner to corner.
One square yields four Side triangles.

To calculate the size to cut Corner Setting triangles, you begin with the finished size of your block and divide by 1.414. Add ⅞'' to that number. Cut a square equal to the sum and cut once, corner to corner.

Example: 6'' blocks   6'' ÷ 1.414 = 4.24 (4¼'')

$4\frac{1}{4}'' + \frac{7}{8}'' = 5\frac{1}{8}''$

Cut a square 5⅛'', cut once

Each square yields two Corner triangles

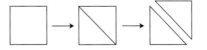

5⅛'' square. Cut once corner to corner.
One square yields two Corner Triangles.

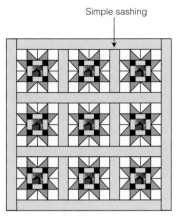

Simple sashing

Straight blocks with simple sashing

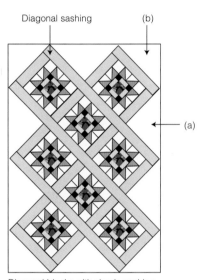

Diagonal sashing   (b)

(a)

Diagonal blocks with simple sashing
(a) Side Setting Triangle (b) Corner Triangle

Sashing

"Sashing" is the strips of fabric used to separate the blocks. You can use sashing with either straight or diagonally oriented blocks. Sashing can be simple, plain strips, or it can be broken into more complex piecing structures. Another term for sashing is "lattice."

NOTE: Once you introduce sashing into the setting equation you also need to be aware of the difference color and value will make to the appearance of the same blocks. Be sure to study the photographs in Chapter 3, page 23, where the same blocks were auditioned with various colors for sashing.

NOTE: When using sashing with the diagonal set your Setting Triangle sizes will change. The number you start your calculation with is equal to the finished size of the block plus the finished width of the sashing; one sashing width for Side triangles, two sashing widths for Corner triangles.

Example: 6" blocks with 1½" sashing

SIDE TRIANGLES: $6'' + 1\frac{1}{2}'' = 7\frac{1}{2}''$ (7.5")
                       $7.5'' \times 1.414 = 10.6''$ (10⅝")*
                       $10\frac{5}{8}'' + 1\frac{1}{4}'' = 11\frac{7}{8}''$
                       Cut a square 11⅞", cut twice corner to corner

* Round decimal number up to the nearest eighth of an inch to keep numbers quilter friendly. See page 12 for Decimal Equivalents Chart.

CORNER TRIANGLES: $6'' + 3'' = 9''$
                       $9'' \div 1.414 = 6.36''$ (6⅜")
                       $6\frac{3}{8}'' + \frac{7}{8}'' = 7\frac{1}{4}''$
                       Cut a square 7¼", cut once corner to corner

TIP *A guideline for the size to make simple sashing strips is ¼th the finished block size. So, a 6" finished block works well with 1½" finished sashing strips. Remember that this is not a rule, but a place to start. What you are looking for is a quilt that feels well balanced. Study quilts and notice the proportion of sashing to blocks. Determine what looks harmonious to you.*

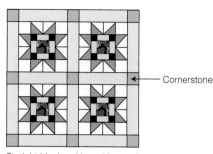

Straight blocks with sashing and cornerstones

Cornerstones

Cornerstones are often, though not always, used with sashing strips. Cornerstones are the squares you see when sashing intersects at a corner and a different fabric is used. Cornerstones can simplify the assembling of the quilt top, as they allow for registration between the rows. A cornerstone is a great place to introduce an accent color.

Alternate Set

An "alternate set" is created when your Focus blocks alternate with another square. That square can be a plain, solid piece of fabric or a different pieced block. The alternate pieced block can range from very simple Nine-Patches and Snowballs to much more involved blocks. (See Chapter 6, Alternating Possibilities, page 45, for some great examples of this set.)

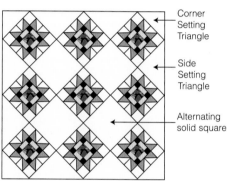

— Corner Setting Triangle

— Side Setting Triangle

— Alternating solid square

Diagonal alternate set with solid squares

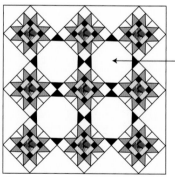

Snowball connector block

Diagonal alternate set with Snowball connector blocks

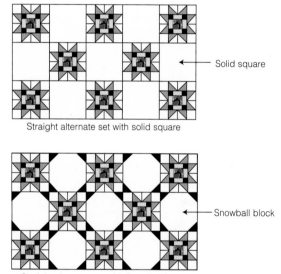

— Solid square

Straight alternate set with solid square

— Snowball block

Straight alternate set with Snowball block

NOTE: The Straight Alternate set needs an odd number (3, 5, 7, or 9, e.g.) of blocks each direction in order for the balance of the quilt to be complete. You want each row to start and end with the same kind of block. The quilt can start with either the focus or the alternating square in the corners.

Putting your blocks on the wall in each of the basic layouts is a good starting point. You might even take photos of your blocks in each mock-up for better comparisons later. Study the mock-ups in the color chapter and audition different colors with your blocks. It can be fun to start a workbook/photo album to store the photos for future reference. Often a setting that doesn't work for one set of blocks can be a great solution for another set of blocks. Having the photos for reference is a fabulous visual tool.

Bonus Decimal Equivalents Chart

DECIMAL EQUIVALENTS

.03125	=	1/32	.2813	=	9/32	.53125	=	17/32	.75	=	3/4
.0625	=	1/16	.3	=	3/10	.5625	=	9/16	.78125	=	25/32
.09375	=	3/32	.3125	=	5/16	.5714	=	4/7	.8	=	4/5
.1	=	1/10	.3333	=	1/3	.59375	=	19/32	.8125	=	13/16
.125	=	1/8	.34375	=	11/32	.6	=	3/5	.833	=	5/6
.1428	=	1/7	.375	=	3/8	.625	=	5/8	.84375	=	27/32
.15625	=	5/32	.4	=	2/5	.65625	=	21/32	.8571	=	6/7
.1666	=	1/6	.40625	=	13/32	.6666	=	2/3	.875	=	7/8
.1875	=	3/16	.4285	=	3/7	.6875	=	11/16	.9	=	9/10
.2	=	1/5	.4375	=	7/16	.7	=	7/10	.90625	=	29/32
.21875	=	7/32	.46875	=	15/32	.7142	=	5/7	.9375	=	15/16
.25	=	1/4	.5	=	1/2	.71875	=	23/32	.96875	=	31/32

This chart can be used any time you are using a calculator to determine sizes and need to convert the decimal number to a more quilter friendly fraction.
Round decimal number up to the nearest eighth of an inch.

Bonus Setting Triangle Chart

BLOCK OR BLOCK PLUS SASHING SIZE	SQUARE SIZE TO CUT FOR SIDE TRIANGLES	SQUARE SIZE TO CUT FOR CORNER TRIANGLES
6"	9¾"	5⅛"
6½"	10½"	5½"
7"	11¼"	5⅞"
7½"	11⅞"	6¼"
8"	12⅝"	6⅝"
8½"	13⅜"	7"
9"	14"	7¼"
9½"	14¾"	7⅝"
10"	15½"	8"
10½"	16⅛"	8⅜"
11"	16⅞"	8¾"
11½"	17⅝"	9"
12"	18¼"	9⅜"
12½"	19"	9¾"
13"	19¾"	10⅛"
13½"	20⅜"	10½"
14"	21⅛"	10⅞"
14½"	21¾"	11⅛"
15"	22½"	11½"
15½"	23¼"	11⅞"
16"	23⅞"	12¼"
16½"	24⅝"	12⅝"
17"	25⅜"	13"
17½"	26"	13¼"
18"	26¾"	13⅝"
18½"	27½"	14"

This chart can be used to determine the size to cut for Setting triangles.

CHAPTER TWO

Reconciling Size Differences

No matter how carefully you cut and piece your blocks, discrepancies among the sizes of the finished blocks inevitably occur. It can happen when all the blocks are the same pattern; it is very likely to happen when you are making different blocks, as in the case of a sampler quilt. And it always happens when different quiltmakers are involved, as in guild block-of-the-month, block party, and friendship exchanges.

I know that there are way too many blocks lying around that haven't made it into quilts because of this size dilemma. But size differences are easy to correct. If the differences are minor—less than 1/4" on blocks between 10 and 12 inches—you can often make them fit by fudging or easing the seams; fabric, after all, is forgiving. But if you try to ease or stretch too much, you run the risk of creating "wonky" quilts. I know you can "quilt it out", but making all the blocks the same size to begin with is a much nicer solution.

There are three ways to make blocks all the same size.
1. You can remake the blocks.
2. You can trim the blocks to make them equal.
3. You can add a frame around all or some of the blocks.

Remaking the Block

Remaking the block is my least favorite method, but it is a good choice when most of the blocks are exactly the same size and only one is considerably larger or smaller. It is often easier to fix one block than it is to adapt several. You might also choose to make one totally new block from scratch, rather than picking apart and re-sewing one. If you do decide to remake a block, be very careful not to stretch and distort the pieces as you unsew it. Check each piece for accuracy in the original cutting before beginning to sew those same pieces of fabric back together. If the pieces were cut incorrectly to begin with, you won't be able to fix the problem until the pieces are right.

Trimming the Block Down

Trimming down works well when points (such as star points) are not involved. Perfect candidates for trimming down might include Nine-Patches, Log Cabins, Four-Patches, and any other block with just squares and rectangles around the outer edges.

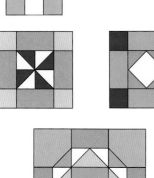

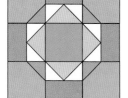

Perfect blocks for trimming down

Tea Basket Challenge, 1999, 64'' x 64''
Sharyn Craig, quilted by Joanie Keith

These blocks were the result of a guild block-of-the-month. They were supposed to be 10½'' square from raw edge to raw edge, but in reality they measured between 9¾'' and 11''. There was a lot of background behind the basket handle, so I was able to square them up by trimming away from primarily this section of the block. The basic design was still intact, and it was so much easier to construct the quilt top with blocks that were all the same size.

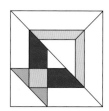

Tea Basket block – before

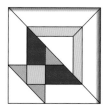

Tea Basket block – after
Red shaded area illustrates how block could be reduced – evened up without sacrificing any design features.

Many blocks can be trimmed without disturbing their basic structure. Spend a few minutes analyzing your block to see if you could trim without compromising the integrity of the block. Such was the case in the Tea Basket blocks you see in this quilt.

The easiest method for squaring up your blocks is to use a large square plexi-ruler. These square rulers come in a variety of sizes. If you don't own one, I suggest buying the largest size you can find. Look for a ruler with measuring lines every ¼'' and numbers at least every inch.

Before you do anything else, be sure to press the block well. Place the pressed block on your cutting mat. If you are right-handed, it is most comfortable to trim the right side and top edge of the block first. Position the ruler on the block so that the "1's" on the ruler are in the top right hand corner of the block. If you are left-handed, it is more comfortable to trim from the left and top; rotate the ruler so the "1's" are in the upper left corner of the block.

Determine the final trimmed size (finished size plus ½'' for seams) of all the blocks, remembering that they must match the smallest block in the collection. Calculate half the trimmed size so you can trim the block evenly (half the trimmed size of an 8½'' block is 4¼'').

Folding the block to be trimmed in fourths and creasing the center position and the center side points.

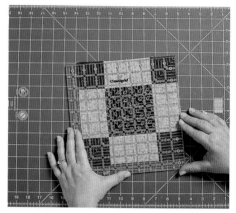

Positioning the plexi-ruler for trimming a block. The photo shows a right-handed ruler position.

Different ways an original block might appear in framing triangles.

Trimmed exactly to ¼'' from edge

Trimmed with lots of triangle remaining

Place the ruler so that the measurement of half the final block size (4¼'' for our example) is in the center of the block, and the fold registration marks align with the correct numbers on the ruler.

Trim away the excess fabric beyond the top and right edges of the ruler. To trim the two remaining sides, turn the block and align the edges you just cut with lines on the ruler indicating your desired block size, and trim away the excess fabric. In our example, the block is aligned at 8½''.

You can sometimes use the trimming down method even with blocks that have points around the outer edge. If the blocks have no points due to faulty construction, then losing a little more by trimming might not matter to you. If the blocks have points properly positioned ¼'' from the edge of the block, trimming can jeopardize them. There will be quilts in this book that sacrificed points for ease of construction, and unless I point it out to you, I guarantee you would never notice it.

Adding a Frame

Adding a frame to the original block is the most flexible of the options and perhaps the easiest. Because I think of this method as a way to cope with the problem with minimal effort and loss to the original block, I call these added pieces "coping" pieces. They can be in the form of strips or triangles. The strips can be simple strips or twisted strips. These frames offer the opportunity to add color and design elements while at the same time equalizing the block sizes.

Simple Coping Triangles

Simple coping triangles are nothing more than oversized triangles. They allow you to make the block really big and then trim it down. An easy way to do this is to cut two squares the same size as the block you are going to frame. Next, cut these squares once diagonally, corner to corner. Sew the resulting triangles to the original block.

To add coping triangles to your block, stitch triangles to two opposite sides of the block. Press carefully, then add triangles to the remaining two sides.

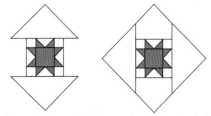

Sewing order for adding over-sized triangles to block

Press the block before squaring it up. Trim as much as you want from the outer edge of the framed blocks. You can allow the corners of the original block to touch the edges (remember, you need to allow ¼'' seams beyond the block corner for sewing the blocks together), or you can make them appear to float by leaving behind as much of the coping triangle as desired.

Adding strips
Log Cabin style

Adding strips
alternating sides

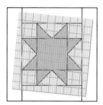

Angle the square-up
ruler on the framed
block to give your
block a twist.

Twisted coping strips

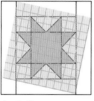

Ruler is positioned to
create less of an angle.

The less you angle your
ruler, the less twist the
block will have.

Left twist

Right twist

Angling the ruler to
the right, results in
left twisting blocks.

Angling the ruler to
the left, results in right
twisting blocks.

Simple Coping Strips

The strips can be any width you want, but I have found that strips cut between 2'' and 3½'' wide are very easy to work with and allow for flexibility of size differences. I definitely recommend that you cut strips wider than you anticipate needing.

You can either add strips in a Log Cabin fashion, going clockwise or counter-clockwise around the block, or add them to two opposite sides first, then to the other two opposite sides.

You can add two or more coping strips around a block if you desire. You can even combine blocks which have one coping strip with blocks with two or more coping strips. This is an excellent solution if your blocks are significantly different in size. Sewing several narrower coping strips, around the smaller blocks, rather than one wide strip can often be more pleasing to the viewer's eye.

Twisted Coping Strips

If, after adding the coping strips, you use your square-up ruler at an angle from the edges of the strips when you even up the blocks, they will appear to twist. How much angle you give the ruler will affect how much "twist" the block gets. You do not have to angle the ruler the same amount each time, or even in the same direction. Angling the ruler to the right during trimming will make the blocks twist left, and vice versa.

Twisting can create a quilt with a lot of movement and design interest. An example of twisted coping strips is *Asilomar Logs*, shown on page 17.

Positive and Negative Coping Pieces

These coping pieces can appear in two different forms: negative or positive. Negative coping pieces disappear; they blend into the quilt. One way to create this negative visibility is to select coping fabrics that match the fabrics they are next to. When the coping fabric matches the background of the block, it becomes a part of the block. On the other hand, when it matches the sashing strip, it identifies with that element. In either situation, the coping strip has become invisible and has what I call "negative visibility."

Positive frames are ones you can see. They contrast, either in color or in value, with the block. If there is just a little contrast, I refer to them as "accent." If the coping fabric has a lot of contrast, they become a dominant part of the quilt. Think of these as "power bars".

Many of the quilts in this book have coping strips. Study the pictures and read the captions. In some quilts you will find that it's almost impossible to see the coping strips, while others make no secret of the fact that the strips are present. You can use the technique of coping strips and triangles to add interest, even if you aren't fixing a size discrepancy between blocks.

Asilomar Logs, 1997, 66" x 66"
Sharyn Craig, quilted by Joanie Keith

I framed the star blocks twice (a double twist). I squared up after each frame, creating the twist. The final blocks finished 12½"x 12½" which was equal in size to the Half Log Cabin blocks. I planned to cut some of the framed star blocks in half for the outside edges. Those blocks were trimmed to 12½" x 13" to allow for the extra seam allowance. Each half-block piece would measure 12½" x 6½".

North Star, 1997, 68" x 68"
Sharyn Craig

The *North Star* quilt is a good example of negative visibility. You can't see the coping strips. I did one additional thing, which also helped camouflage the coping strips. After I framed (with coping strips), I then pressed and squared the blocks. Next, I cut away the corners of the framed blocks and added new triangles (Read the information on Corner Cutters starting on page 65 for an easy way to do this). The added triangles were a way to introduce other colors and fool your eye into not noticing the coping strips.

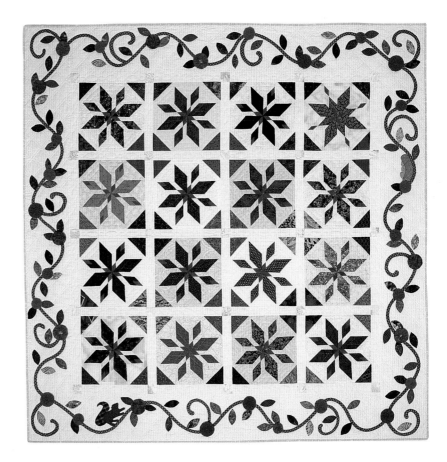

Festival Chain, 1998, 64" x 64"
Sharyn Craig, quilted by Joanie Keith
Project Map, page 82

Festival Chain is yet another example of negative visibility coping strips. This time the coping strip matched the base of the yellow triangle found in the pieced sashing. You will notice that the coping strips are definitely not the same size from block to block. The coping strips played another very valuable role in the creation of this quilt. The original stars were 11" blocks, but the alternating blocks were 12". By framing each of the focus blocks with extra wide yellow strips, I was then able to square them up to 12½", the exact size of the alternating block.

The Trouble With Purple, 1999, 57" x 57"
Sharyn Craig
Project Map, page 83

The trouble with purple is that it is just that: **purple**. Even if you like purple, which I do, you might not particularly want a purple quilt. Personally, I don't think this quilt reads purple. I think it reads as primarily black, red, and yellow, with purple accents. Once again, the fabric used to frame each Focus block matches the triangle in the sashing next to it. Careful color positioning of the red triangles creates the secondary pinwheel design. Did you even notice that the block in the very center of the quilt is not the same pattern as the other eight blocks? Not only that, but it was a 10" original block, while the other blocks were 9". Why is the center block different than the others? Because I only had eight of the one kind. Sure, I could have made one more block, but how great that I didn't have to and was able to use an orphan block that didn't have another home (Read more about orphan blocks and their fun resolutions in Chapter 7).

Ohio Star Plus, 1998, 62" x 62"
Sharyn Craig

My *Ohio Star Plus* quilt illustrates the use of accent coping strips. If you look closely at the quilt, you will notice that only six of the blocks have coping strips. The fabrics selected for the strips were chosen to accent rather than overpower. There are both 7½" and 9" blocks in the body of this quilt. Adding coping strips to the 7½" blocks and squaring them up to match the larger blocks allowed all to fit together easily. One of the 9" blocks was bigger than all the other blocks, so I decided to trim it down, even though it meant sacrificing points. See if you can find the culprit.

In addition to having six 7½" blocks and seven 9" blocks, I also found a great way to work two 6" blocks into the quilt. Can you find them? Look at the four corners of the pieced setting triangles. I sliced each of the 6" blocks in half diagonally and used the half star as the corner setting triangles.

Are you shocked? Don't be. You are allowed to cut your blocks any way you want. After all, trimming down was one of the options for reconciling size differences. Slicing them in half is a very loose interpretation of the trimming down concept, but it works, and in this situation very nicely.

We will talk more about color in the next chapter, but you might be interested to know that it was red, black, and yellow 6" blocks, which determined the color for the entire quilt. The other blocks are every color combination you can imagine.

Celebration, 1994, 58" x 73"
Sharyn Craig, quilted by Phyllis Reddish

Celebration is an example of power bar coping strips that twist. Any time you make a sampler quilt (every block a different pattern), you run into the problem of blocks turning out different sizes. One problem we frequently have when making sampler quilts is achieving balance between the scale and patterns of the various blocks. One way to unify a collection of sampler blocks is to select colors that are so strong that they pull the random blocks together. The selection of strong, graphic colors definitely created the party-like atmosphere for these blocks.

Radiant Star, 1996, 74" x 74"
Arlene Stamper, quilted by Lori Mayne

The fourteen blocks were the result of a friendship exchange. There is no way fourteen different people can make the same block and have them all come out the same size! Therefore, Arlene selected the nine blocks closest in size for the central body of her quilt and cut the remaining blocks into quarters. She used those quartered triangles to create the pieced framing border for the rest of the blocks. Yes, she lost points. Yes, she sacrificed seam allowances. But, wow! What a stunning quilt. Our ancestors cut up blocks all the time: now it is our turn.

Playful Garden, 2000, 94" x 106"
Sharyn Craig.
Mini Project Map, page 87

Here is one more quilt that combined several different things. First, some of the blocks were 9" and some were 6". I used oversized coping triangles on each of the 6" blocks and squared them up to be 9½" . Next I framed every single block with the same green fabric strips and squared them up. The coping strips could be considered negative visibility, because they actually became the setting structure for the blocks. You will find an easy way to construct the sashing pieces in Chapter 8, and a detailed illustration for piecing structure on page 87.

To sum up, size reconciliation can be accomplished in three basic ways:
- You can elect to totally take the block apart and remake it.
- You can trim the blocks down to the needed size to make the block sizes equal.
- You can add to the basic blocks in the form of strips or triangles to create new equal sized blocks.

It is obviously difficult to separate the problems of color and size when making a quilt, since they are both so essential to the end result. In this chapter the goal was to present options for reconciling size differentials between blocks. After you have read and digested the information in the next chapter on Color Correction, please come back to this chapter. Study the quilts again for the effect that color choices have played in the final outcome.

CHAPTER THREE

Color Correction

Color is the first thing you notice about any quilt you see. You are excited by colors you like and turned off by colors that you don't care for. Often, even though we know what we like, we don't understand what actually happens with color and why we react as we do. In general, trouble with color is the number one problem quilters think they have and that they need help with.

What if I told you that all colors go together? It's true. Just walk outside and look around you. Study the flowers in the garden, the way the sky caresses the ground, a sunset. You can learn a lot from your surroundings, especially when you realize which ones make you the most comfortable. Do you prefer the bright, cheerful profusion of spring flowers, or the cool gentleness of a winter day? How about the texture of a forest in the fall—is this a positive feeling for you?

Color Theory

If you went back to school and took some art theory classes, one of the things that you would learn is that all colors go together. There are four basic classifications for the way colors go together.

1 One such category is *adjacent*, or *analogous*. This means the colors appear next to one another on the color wheel. Red and orange are adjacent colors.

2 The second category is the *monochromatic*. Mono means one. A monochromatic quilt would be all one color. An example would be one created all in varieties of blue.

3 The third way to label color schemes is *complementary*. Complements appear directly across from one another on the color wheel. Complementary color schemes include red and green, blue and orange, or yellow and purple.

4 The fourth general category is *polychromatic*, meaning all colors. Most scrap quilts are polychromatic.

I grant you that this is a very simplified version of color theory and there are many sub-categories of these headings, but the fact remains: the more you study color the more you will begin to realize that all colors go together.

Just because colors go together does not mean that you have to like them all. But if you can accept that you don't need help learning about which colors do go together, we can get on with the more important issues that you should learn about: value, intensity, temperature, print pattern, print scale and proportion. These are the culprit areas, the subjects that confuse, overwhelm, frustrate, and basically give you trouble in your quilts.

Value

Value simply means how light or dark a color, or in our case a fabric, appears. You need to remember that this factor is determined by what a given fabric's neighbors are. It is possible that the same fabric could appear light in one position and dark in another. It is easy to take a piece of a pale blue fabric and assume it is light. However, position it next to white, and it suddenly appears dark. Conversely, place it next to black and it appears light.

Intensity

Intensity is the amount of brightness or dullness. A blue-gray fabric is dull; therefore we say it is one of low intensity. The clear blue that you might use on a child's primary colored quilt would be classified as bright, or having high intensity. Too many dull fabrics used together can wash out a quilt. Too many bright fabrics might be too busy.

Temperature

Temperature refers to how warm or cool a color appears. In general, reds, yellows, and oranges are the warm colors, while the blues, greens, and purples are cooler. Warmer colors advance, while cooler ones recede.

Warmer colors can appear lighter and airier, while cooler ones can be heavier and calmer.

Print pattern

Unless you are using solids (fabrics with no pattern), your fabrics have designs on them that range from very small to quite large in scale. Prints can be monochromatic, such as a tone-on-tone, or they can be multi-colored. We are often drawn to the same types of patterns in our fabric selections. We need to learn how to successfully combine a variety of patterns in different scales. Too many of the same type of prints creates a busy and often disturbing look in a finished quilt.

Proportion

Proportion is the amount of any of the above mentioned areas present at the same time. Go back into the garden. Is there an exact 50/50 mix of red and green? No. There is more of one color than there is of the other. This same thing is true in quilts. A quilt that is exactly 50% white and 50% black would make your eyes vibrate way too much. This proportion factor holds true for intensity, print scale, temperature, etc. Look at the antique, two-color quilts and see how our grandmothers successfully worked with proportion in relationship to value.

Personal preference

There is another thing that has to be factored into this equation: your personal preference. What kinds of quilts do you like? Do you like high or low contrast quilts? A high contrast quilt has obvious pattern and strong delineation between the components. A low contrast quilt has much softer and more subtle differences between the various fabrics and shapes.

Look at pictures of quilts, study them at a quilt show, analyze your own, and try to determine which ones you like better. Next, try to determine why you like certain quilts. One technique that might help is to assign adjectives such as feminine, masculine, whimsical, warm, sad, strong, or busy to the quilt you are viewing. As you assign various adjectives to different quilts, you will have reactions to those words. Identifying the feeling the quilt generates is one way to start knowing which ones work for you.

As you study the quilts, concentrate on the topics I have introduced here. Think about the amount of contrast you see, the brightness or dullness of the colors. Study the actual color. Once you know where you feel the most content you will be on your way towards solving your color problems. There are some excellent books on color for quilters. I have listed some at the end of this chapter if you want more in-depth treatments of this subject. Now it is time to leave the textbook approach and come at the subject from a totally different angle.

Color Preferences

Most quilters make and like a variety of quilts. I love red and green quilts and prefer high contrast quilts in bright, clear colors, however I do make other types of quilts. I am not crazy about orange, peach and rust—basically any derivative of orange—so why would I deliberately choose to work in those colors? For the most part, I don't. But that doesn't mean I never encounter orange in the blocks I have to work with. Now we are getting to the real meat of this chapter. How can you turn blocks you don't care for, color-wise, into a quilt that you like, or even love?

From time to time, almost every quilter has had to face this challenge. The reasons you have these blocks can be exactly the same as we talked about in the previous chapter on size reconciliation. It can happen when you make the blocks yourself, and it is probably going to happen when other people make the blocks.

Block Dilemma

Blocks that we don't like are a problem. But we have them, and we want to get them into a quilt. You don't want to spend time, energy, and money working on a quilt you are not going to like any better than you like the blocks you have right now. Is there any solution for this dilemma? You bet there is.

These next statements may amaze you, but read them, think about them, look at the quilts throughout this book, and then accept them:

- You can make the finished quilt in different colors than the original blocks.

- If you don't like the types of prints used in the original blocks, you don't have to stay with that style of print.

- If the original blocks are low contrast and you like high contrast, or vice-versa, your final quilt can achieve that effect.

- If the original blocks were made with dull value colors and you want them to be bright, the final quilt can be clear, bright, and intense (The opposite of this statement is also true).

If you don't like the colors of the original blocks, why would you even consider putting more of those colors in the quilt? Years ago some people felt that you had to use one of the fabrics from the blocks as the border. I have no idea why or how this belief started, but many of us have heard it. Forget it.

Often, these intense beliefs feel like rules, and the fear of "breaking the rules" sometimes makes us feel we will never get it right.

Remember that there are no rules, only guidelines. If I make a statement that sounds like a rule, remember it is only a guideline. The first thing you need to do is relax. Identifying what you like and don't like allows you to make more educated choices, to fix your quiltmaking problems.

Playing With Color

Next, I want you to watch what happens when I audition some identical blocks on top of various colors to see how they look. To keep this example simple I am only going to play with the straight, sashed set. Audition the blocks on a large piece of fabric, exposing the appropriate amount to represent sashing. What color or colors do you see when you look at one block?

Purple. You see purple, and—oh yes, white. Look again and you will notice the yellow. Get close enough to the print in the center square of the block and you can isolate green, red, and black. It seems the most logical choice for sashing is some value of purple between very light and very dark.

Remember what I said earlier: you can use any colors you want to set your blocks together. Just because there is no blue in the blocks doesn't mean you can't use blue to sash them.

Blocks on blue

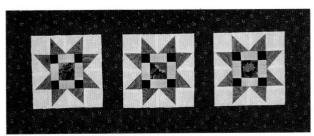

Blocks on purple

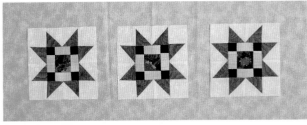

Blocks on yellow

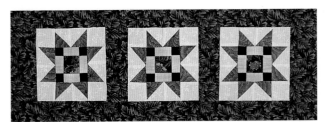

Blocks on green

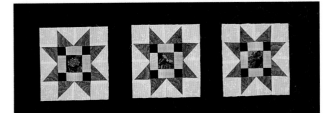

Blocks on black

Blocks on red

Yellow. Green. Black. Any color you want. What if you used all of the colors?

The point is simple. Each of these mock-ups works. You probably don't like all of them, but you have to admit that the purple blocks can be sashed with any of the colors. Color is a personal thing. I can tell you something is correct and that it works, but I can't make you like it.

Don't be afraid to audition your blocks with different colors. Look for the obvious, then the not-so-obvious. It can be fun to ask a total stranger for their opinion. In the quilt shop, look around, show someone your blocks, and ask for a suggestion. You don't have to take the suggestion, but it is fun to play. Strangers have no preconceived notion of what you will like.

Blocks on combination of purple, blue, red, yellow, green and black

Sue's Bees 1999, 63" x 80" Sharyn Craig, quilted by Gem Taylor. Owned by Sue Chapel

In 1985, seventeen of Sue's friends each made a Honey Bee block for her. Sue picked the gray pin dot and the light calico print for each person to use, and each friend selected another print to complete the block. As expected, the blocks were not the same size, and Sue didn't know how to fix the problem, so the blocks sat in a dresser drawer until 1999. When Sue found them all those years later, she knew she could fix the size problem, but by then she didn't like the calico prints or colors used. Always ready for a challenge, I asked Sue if I could work with the blocks.

Since I know Sue's favorite color is blue, the selection of the blue fabric was natural. I selected a blue tonal to calm down the vibrations from the multi-colored calicos and a soft peach tonal for the second fabric. Seventeen blocks are not easy to put together into one quilt, but careful, strategic positioning of the focus blocks made it possible.

One definitely gets a sense of calm and peace when looking at this quilt. The dynamics of the alternating block echo the diagonal line created by the appliquéd bees. The overall pattern is created with a simple alternating square split diagonally and colored half light and half dark. Note that four of the blocks have been modified to allow the pattern to change directions.

Blue was chosen simply because it is Sue's favorite color. But honestly, any color would have worked with these blocks. The overall quilt reads blue because of that one fabric. Look what happens when we digitally alter the blue triangles and make them appear purple; then green; then red. Amazing isn't it?

When purple fabric "replaced" the blue in the alternating blocks and border the result is now a purple quilt.

Use green fabric instead of blue and you have a green quilt.

Red fabric definitely creates a red quilt.

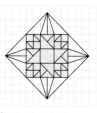

Iced Stars, 1999, 47" x 57"
Barbara Hutchins, quilted by Joanie Keith

Single block in the
triangle frame

Note: Shaded area = Focus block
What if you substituted a different block?
What is in your stash?

Now, let us look at Barbara Hutchin's dramatic *Iced Stars*. It began as a stack of fourteen blue star variation blocks from a friendship exchange and a single oval lavender Mariner's Compass block. Barbara didn't want a blue quilt. Her goal: lose the blue.

Barbara decided to over-dye the blocks in a light red-violet dye bath. That's right—she took the blocks and plunged them into the colored water. She chose that dye color because of the oval compass block, but she could have used any color. After careful rinsing and pressing, the blocks were ready for the next phase.

Barbara's next challenge was to reconcile size. She opted to trim down those few blocks that were too big. She then put pieced framing triangles around each of the original blocks.

NOTE: You will find additional discussion on this subject on page 34, Framing the Competition.

Once the size of these new blocks was determined, she knew how much she had to add to the Mariner's Compass in order for everything to fit. Simple strips were used to fill the space. The simple framing strips were repeated at the outer edge to finish the quilt.

NOTE: Check for the cross-reference to other quilts on page 91, made from these very same blue blocks. The difference in color in the various finished quilts is truly amazing,

Joanie's Patriotic, 1998, 45" x 64"
Sharyn Craig, quilted and owned by Joanie Keith

In *Joanie's Patriotic*, the original Focus blocks were red, off-white, and blue. The colors for the coping strips were deliberately selected to overwhelm the original blocks. Joanie had stopped making blocks when she got to seven because, frankly, she didn't like them.

Joanie said I could do anything I wanted to. Knowing that Joanie's least favorite color was red, the decision was made to not use more red in setting the blocks together. The original colors were very dull in value. I selected bright fabrics in green, yellow, hot pink, orange, and blue. It didn't matter that those colors weren't present in the original blocks.

Seven blocks is not an easy number of blocks to put together. First the blocks were framed with no rhyme or reason—just whatever caught my fancy. Next the blocks were put on point. By creating pieced side and corner triangles with repeats of the colors, I added another point of design interest to the equation. The goal was to lose the original blocks while creating a quilt that made both of us feel good. The final result is a whimsical, charming, fun quilt that challenges the viewer to even find the original red, blue, and off-white blocks.

Coloring for Fun, 1999, 55" x 55"
Nancy Nichols

You have seen some of these blocks before. On page 18, my quilt, *The Trouble with Purple*, had eight of these very same blocks. Nancy turned her blocks into a very cheerful, vibrant, fun explosion of color. Her goal was to tone down the amount of red-violet in the original blocks. Introducing the yellow definitely warmed up the quilt. Using warm greens and warm blues along with some more red-violet completed the fabric color recipe. This quilt would definitely feel good on a gray, rainy day.

Before we leave this chapter on color correction, I don't want you to think that I am telling you that you have to do something different with the colors you use. If you are happy with the colors you work with, the blocks you have set, and the finished feeling you are achieving in your quilts, then do not change.

If you would like to study the subject of color in greater depth, I highly recommend the following books:

Color Play by Joen Wolfrom
Color Confidence for Quilters by Jinny Beyer
Color and Cloth by Mary Coyne Penders
Ideas for Color and Fabric by Susan McElvey

Dare to be Different

What do I mean when I say, "dare to be different"? Assume you have always made a quilt as the result of a pattern, a workshop, a picture, or a magazine. Someone else made choices for you about how many fabrics you used and the amount of each fabric, what block you were making, etc. You knew, before you began, what the quilt was going to look like. What if you don't have a pattern? You would be taking a risk, not knowing what it will look like. Well, I dare you.

I dare you to make yourself—and your quilt—vulnerable to that opportunity. Notice the use of the word "opportunity." If you think of this as an opportunity, instead of a risk, your entire mind-set will change, and you might even enjoy the process.

It can be incredibly rewarding to make a quilt unlike any you have ever seen before. I know it isn't easy. When working this way, every quilt I make has the possibility of "failure"—of not turning out like I had hoped. But, then, every quilt also has the potential of becoming something really great.

What is the worst thing that could possibly happen if you take this chance? Maybe you would have invested some time, fabric, and money into a quilt, that, instead of turning out wonderful, becomes something you would rather donate to some charitable cuddle quilt project.

You might think of this chapter as the start of "being on your own". I hope to introduce you to some tools you can use to initiate this process. I hope you will see that different solutions are possible, and those will help make you an independent quiltmaker.

You don't have to make Ohio Stars to use the set I did in *Ohio Stars Plus* on page 46. You don't have to make some blue blocks to make a quilt like *It Takes a Village* on page 32. You do have to start thinking about how to translate your blocks into your quilt. I hope that you will be inspired by some of these quilts, but you don't have to make a quilt exactly like any of the ones you see here.

First you find a quilt you like, and might want to work with, then you challenge yourself to change it. If we are going to talk about change, you need to understand the ingredients so you know what can be changed. Do you understand the properties of a quilt? Color is one obvious property. When you are at a quilt show, you will actually "not see" certain quilts because of the way you react to certain colors. If you love red, you will see every red quilt at the show, but you will skip right over the purple ones if purple is not your thing.

Pattern is another property of a quilt. Some people love stars and will see every star quilt hanging in the show, while other people prefer all-over designs such as Log Cabins, Kaleidoscopes, or Pineapples.

The set of the blocks is another property of a quilt. Are the blocks tangent, alternating, sashed? What is the orientation of the blocks? Are they straight or on-point? Does the quilt have a border? Does it have multiple borders? What is the scale of the pattern? Are all blocks the same size?

The bottom line is that you have these basic properties to make a quilt:

- Color
- Pattern
- Set
- Orientation
- Borders
- Scale

If you are going to make a quilt that is different, you need to challenge yourself to make changes to these properties. The easiest thing to change is the color. Look at any quilt in this book and picture it in another color. Now, look at that same quilt and imagine it with the values (lightness and darkness) reversed. Picture all the light areas now being dark, and vice versa. Even if you can't really "see" this reversal, you might make that your challenge.

Start with simple changes, like reversing the values or changing the colors. Try putting the blocks on point if the original quilt sets the blocks straight. Once you start with simple changes and gain a bit of confidence, you will not be afraid to make more challenging changes.

The quilts in this book are all inspired by other quilts. You don't need to start from scratch with each quilt you make. I frequently make a quilt based on one I just finished, but not wanting to make the same one twice, I pick a single aspect of the quilt to change. When finished, the new piece feels as fresh and as exciting as the first one did.

To illustrate the points I am trying to make in this chapter, I have selected a setting that isn't very common. I have included a body of quilts that each share this same set. These quilts will hopefully make you not only stop and think, but also inspire you to run for your blocks and fabric, so excited that you can't wait to make your next quilt!

First I will explain the "Set". It's really quite simple, but it looks really hard. What occurs is that the blocks have two different kinds of framing. Half of the blocks are framed with straight strips. The other half of the blocks are framed with triangles. I am calling this set 2-for-1.

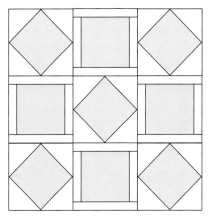

Mini Project Map for basic 2-for-1 set.

This Project Map acts like a blueprint to the quilt. You can insert any block, any size, and any color into the appropriate spaces. When you reduce a quilt to the simple construction lines necessary to hold your blocks together, it definitely takes away a lot of the mystery, doesn't it? Certain fabric choices (such as ones that camouflage seams) can make a quilt look impossible, when they are really unbelievably simple to construct.

Now, let's look at the first quilt using this 2-for-1 set. Linda Packer used the 2-for-1 set on a group of Ohio Star Plus blocks. She started with 9" blocks and 7½" blocks. Each of the 9" blocks was framed with straight strips of the same pink fabric. The 7½" blocks were framed with over-size triangles. All blocks evened-up to the same size. The strip framed blocks are set on the diagonal. The blocks alternate.

PROBLEM: Different sized blocks, no unifying colors in the various blocks

GOAL: Reconcile block-sizes to be uniform while making a quilt with an "old" feel to it.

SOLUTION: Coping strips around nine blocks, coping triangles around the other four blocks. Unification of color in framing pieces establishes tone for the entire quilt to become green and pink, as a throw back to the mid 1800's.

Ohio Stars and More, 1998, 57" x 57"
Linda Packer

Light Show 1998, 56" x 56"
Sharyn Craig

What would happen if we sub-divided the framing strips and triangles? Simple lines have been added to both the straight strips and the triangles. Looking at this next quilt, you can see how a combination of structural lines and coloring choices makes it appear to be a totally different set.

PROBLEM: Different sized blocks, blocks needed color unification.

GOAL: Fix size and color so a child's play quilt could be made.

SOLUTION: Coping strips and triangles. Once added, the blocks could be evened up to be the same size. Bright clear primary colors make a whimsical and child-like palette.

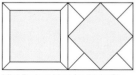

Mini Project Map for *Light Show*

In *Simple Gifts*, the four corner squares have strips only on the two outside edges. The center block has straight stripping all the way around the block. The remaining blocks have plain triangles, but notice that color plays a very special role in the overall design of this quilt. By coloring the eight inside triangles a darker value than the outside ones, we create a large secondary star image. You do not have to treat all blocks the same.

PROBLEM: Size and color of blocks

GOAL: Use 2-for-1 set, but make the quilt look very different from others

SOLUTION: Coping strips were added to only 2 sides of the blocks then squared up. Careful consideration given to fabric color choices to create secondary star design with the coping triangles.

Square with strips on only two sides. Who says the framing strips have to be all the way around the block? Feel free to add strips to just two sides of the block.

Simple Gifts, 1999, 47'' x 47'',
Sharyn Craig, quilted by Joanie Keith

In order to make these pieces "fit" I added coping strips to the blocks, before I added the pieced strips. I also added coping strips first on the two blocks with pieced triangles. This is the first example of sashing in this set. Do you wonder what this quilt would look like with light sashing instead of dark? I added a piecing line to the side setting triangles, allowing different fabrics to be used. It only takes a little bit more time to piece something like this, and the "wow" factor is worth the effort.

PROBLEM: Size and color

GOAL: Make a quilt for a workshop sample.

SOLUTION: Coping strips added to blocks first, so that they would then fit the piecing structure designed for unification of both size and block pattern. I selected the strong green fabric for sashing color to calm blocks down and make the quilt a bit bigger. Dividing the setting triangles also added pattern and color interest.

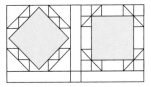

Mini Project Map for *Ripley Star*
Framed block plus sashing

Ripley Star, 1997, 74'' x 56''
Sharyn Craig, quilted by Diane Beaubien

It *Takes a Village* used plain dark strips around twelve of the blocks and pieced triangles to frame the other six.

When using pieced triangles this way, you need to have Focus blocks that are the same, or nearly the same, size. But what if they aren't the same size? How about coping strips first? Negative visibility strips would have been the ideal solution to make blocks all the same size, but not change the design's visual appearance. The blocks came from a swap so more background fabric to match each block would not have been possible. Since the framing triangles were from my stash, I could have framed each block with that light fabric first, squared up the block, then added the pieced triangles.

PROBLEM: Size and color

GOAL: Correct block sizes. Add additional color while retaining tranquil, peaceful feeling.

SOLUTION: Pushed color with addition of greens and purples to keep blocks from being so monochromatic. I achieved size reconciliation with coping strips. The framing triangles were sewn to the blocks most nearly the same size.

It *Takes a Village*, 1996, 56" x 71"
Sharyn Craig, quilted by Joanie Keith
Project Map, page 84

Autumn Splendor, 1996, 60" x 60"
Sharyn Craig, quilted by Joanie Keith
Project Map, page 84

While piecing It *Takes a Village*, I wondered what it would look like if the straight framing strips were light instead of dark. What if the strips weren't solid and I added cornerstones for a different look? I decided to find out using a set of Eddystone Light blocks from yet another friendship exchange. I wanted one more change. I designed a different pieced structure for the framing triangles.

PROBLEM: Color. Too much orange in blocks.

GOAL: Make a quilt in fall colors, but minimize the orange. Also—to use the 2-for-1 set in a different coloration to alter the final results.

SOLUTION: To offset the strong orange feeling of the blocks. I chose colors from the cooler side of the color wheel to work with, especially green and purple.

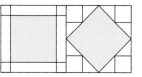

Mini Project Map for *Autumn Splendor*

Barbara's Transparencies,
1999, 54'' x 54''
Barbara Hutchins,
quilted by Joanie Keith

Barbara used coping strips first to reconcile size for all the blocks. She used solid triangles to frame five blocks, but she chose to piece triangles in the straight strip location. Next, Barbara sewed green strips around five blocks and pink strips around the other four. A black-and-white stripe fabric, carefully cut, creates this checkerboard looking effect in the sashing. Barbara didn't have a block for the center of the quilt. She went to her stash and found the flower pot block that fit the size and color scheme. The obvious solution is to find fabric and make another Focus block. Barbara used another approach. This is a great way to use "orphan" blocks.

PROBLEM: One block short, color, and size.

GOAL: Finish quilt for up coming quilt show.

SOLUTION: Substitute one flower pot block, coping strips, and framing triangles. Barbara achieved color reconciliation through the pink and green fabrics, design interest through the black-and-white stripe fabric.

Hard to believe that the seven quilts shown in this chapter all share the same basic set, isn't it? Each of these quilts fits into the same Project Map on page 29. What differs from quilt to quilt is the actual block that was used, the size of the pieces, the color of the pieces, the value of the colors, and even the structure of the strips and triangles. You can do this with any set.

In this chapter, my goal was to teach you how to analyze the quilts you see pictured throughout the book. It is my hope that you will soon start to ask your own "what if?" questions. I will plant the seeds and provide the tools, but it is up to each one of you to take on the challenge and "dare to be different"!

NOTE: One last footnote about the quilts you see in this chapter. Look again at the quilts *It Takes a Village* and *Autumn Splendor* on page 32. Would you believe that I used the exact same border on each of these two quilts? The same. Look at them. Can you see it? Amazing, isn't it? I only changed the colors and the values.

CHAPTER FIVE

Framing the Competition

Sawtooth Star

Windblown Square

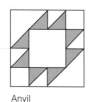

Anvil

Cypress

The focus here is to learn new ways to enhance your blocks. You might have simple Ohio Star blocks to begin with, but they do not have to look so simple when you are done with them. Have you ever thought about positioning your blocks "inside" another traditional block?

There are a lot of traditional blocks that have plain areas in the center. The larger these blocks are, the bigger that plain area is. Some examples of simple blocks that make excellent frames include blocks seen on the left.

A 6'' Sawtooth Star block has a 3'' square in the center. A 12'' Sawtooth Star has a 6'' area in the center. If you have a stack of 6'' Ohio Star blocks you can't decide what to do with, you might consider this possibility for setting them together.

Why would this setting be something you might want to consider?

- It might be worth using for the simple reason that it is unexpected. Doing something different and unexpected is what we are looking for.

- It might be the perfect solution if your blocks are very diverse in color and pattern. Setting sampler blocks inside a common frame can definitely bring unity to diversity. Even scrappy blocks that are all the same pattern could be unified with this solution.

- It might be a great solution if you have a limited number of small blocks but you want a large quilt. Framing blocks in this manner definitely makes them bigger, which in turn leads to a larger finished quilt.

As you choose colors for these frames, you can either keep them very simple and consistent, or make each one different. If the original blocks are extremely busy and scrappy and that busy-ness is bothering you, you can calm them down by selecting fewer fabrics and fewer colors, and always placing values (dark and light) in the same position. On the other hand if your original blocks are boring (dull, flat, lifeless, uninteresting—remember the adjective game I introduced on page 22), then you might elect to punch them up by choosing brighter fabrics and going much scrappier. This goes back to identifying the problem and establishing the goal on pages 5 and 6. Only you can determine which way to solve your problem.

Start with any book that has lots of blocks to look at. Remember that you are looking for a space to fill. But wait a minute—why couldn't we choose an involved block and simply "erase" the middle? You can do anything you want. There are no rules.

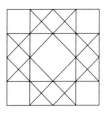

Square and Star block

A

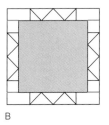

B

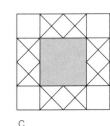

C

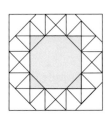

Festival Star block

Festival Star block with corner
triangles shaded to match
octagon, making a square

Shaded areas illustrate different ways Focus blocks can be positioned inside another block.

⬤ **NOTE:** The red lines on option B indicate new construction lines that would be added for ease in sewing.

We have been assuming we need a block with a square in the middle. What about the Festival Star block with its octagon shape?

I first encountered this block when a friend bought an antique quilt at Quilt Festival in Houston, which was made with this block (hence the name I christened it with: Festival Star. Undoubtedly it has another name, but I am partial to this one as it generates fond memories). As I looked at the quilt, my mental wheels started turning with all kinds of "what-if" ideas. All of them related to putting other blocks inside the star frame—that is, replacing the octagon with a different block. Or, you could imagine the four triangles that touch the octagon's corners as being connected to the octagon and you would have a square. You could go either way, finishing a square or an octagon with your Focus blocks inside.

I had a set of 6" LeMoyne Star blocks already made. I drafted the Festival Star block to accommodate the 6" LeMoyne Stars. The new block size is 11".

Sharyn's Festival Star, 1997, 72" x 72"
Sharyn Craig
Project Map for border, page 88

Nancy's *Festival Star* proves that just about any block looks good set inside this frame. The blocks were from an exchange in which the assignment was to replace the plain center with any other interesting block. There was no color recipe given in this exchange, so the blocks were incredibly diverse. Some were very soft and pale, while others were strong and graphic. First Nancy placed 6" blocks inside the Festival Star frame, and those went inside the Pineapple-style blocks. Her transition diagonally across the quilt, from the lightest of greens in the upper left to the darkest in the bottom right-hand corner, creates a wonderful non-traditional feel for the finished quilt.

Nancy's Festival Star, 1998, 66" x 66"
Nancy Nichols

Bonus pieces for an 11" Festival Star frame. These pieces will fit any 6" (finished) Center block.

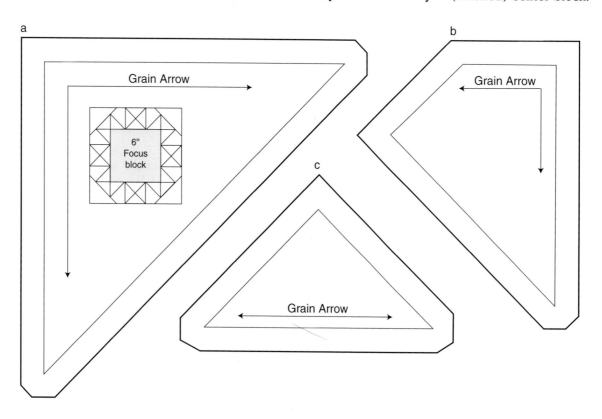

Before I go any further, let's go back to some of the simpler block frames. I certainly do not want you to think you have to use complex blocks and complex frames in order to have this concept work. Windblown Square is a very simple traditional block.

A 12″ Windblown Square would ordinarily be very clumsy looking, but that is definitely not the case when 6″ blocks replace the solid square. The nine LeMoyne Star blocks, leftovers from other projects, were very scrappy. Look closely and you will see red, gold, and even purple stars.

Windblown Square

Windy Stars, 1998, 47″ x 47″
Sharyn Craig, quilted by Joanie Keith.
Project Map, page 85

Inspired by the *Windy Stars* quilt, I made this next whimsical quilt for my granddaughter. This time the Windblown Square blocks are only 6″, which makes the center square 3″. Notice how a different pinwheel shape emerges because of the way the colors run from one block to the next. It was necessary to plan out this entire quilt on the flannel wall first.

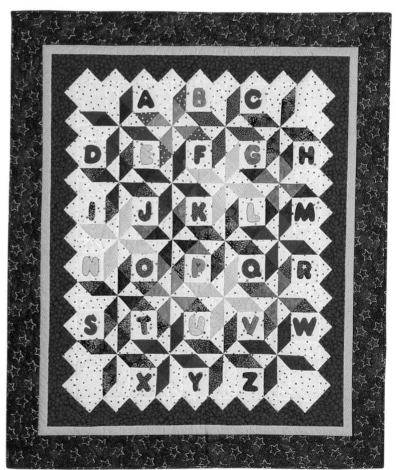

For My Baby, 1999, 48″ x 42″
Sharyn Craig

Star of the Lake, 1998, 60" x 77"
Sharyn Craig, quilted by Joanie Keith

Lady of the Lake

Lady of the Lake is another traditional block with a "hole" in the middle.

The set of blocks I used needed something "different". Lady of the Lake was the perfect solution.

This quilt introduces something else for you to consider. Notice how each of the original blocks has coping strips (accent) before the triangle frame. The coping strips reconciled the size differential between the twelve blocks, but they also made it easy to make the star blocks fit the triangle border. Framing the Focus blocks and squaring them up to be 9" finished blocks (9½" with the seam allowance) made it very easy to determine the sizes for the pieces of the triangle frame. Another solution to this sizing dilemma would have been to modify the Lady of the Lake frame to have four triangles along the side edge.

Just because you frame the blocks with another block doesn't mean you are necessarily finished. The first three quilts took the framed blocks and set them side by side. This one introduced sashing to the equation. You still need to decide how to set the blocks. You have accomplished a totally different look for your original blocks, an increase in size, and an opportunity to standardize color and size.

Margret Reap had some basket blocks from a friendship exchange. Each block was a different pattern, and coloration. Margret wanted something besides a predictable sashed set for her sampler blocks. A very simple block used as a setting frame with simple coloring definitely pulls the blocks together, while at the same time creating a different focus for your eye.

Margret's Basket, 1999, 81" x 81"
Margret Reap
Mini Project Map, page 84

A collection of Sister's Choice blocks from another exchange provided quite a challenge for me. Normally, when we make blocks, we make blocks that we like. However, when we trade blocks with other people, the blocks we receive don't always please us. That was definitely the case here. Some blocks were very light and airy, while others were dark and heavy. There didn't appear to be any color cohesiveness although they were all based on the same floral fabric.

Looking for a way to frame the blocks and give them that unity, I auditioned the Sister's Choice blocks on top of some Radiant Star blocks (You may remember this block seen in Arlene Stamper's quilt page 20).

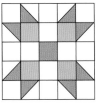

Sister's Choice

Radiant Star

Sister's Star, 1995, 92'' x 70''
Sharyn Craig, quilted by Diane Beaubien

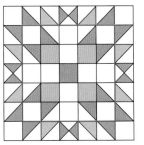

Sister's Choice block on top of one Radiant Star block

It took time to cut and piece all the triangle frames for the blocks, but the end result was new blocks that satisfied me. Once the blocks were framed, I set them on point with additional pieced triangle frames.

The original plan was to have each of the four framing triangles be identical. In fact, I made them that way. But a few minutes of playing "Fruit Basket Upset" (moving the framing triangles all around on the wall) created a much more unexpected result. The first way was safe, controlled, ordinary, expected. Playing with the pieces prior to setting them together with the focus blocks only took a few minutes. Allowing yourself to play with your blocks this way, free from the original "recipe", can be so exciting.

Original recipe for framing triangles

A set of the G blocks gave Laurine Leeke a big challenge (See page 92 for an explanation of this exchange). The blocks were strong and very purple, but Laurine prefers softer colors. Using the simple Log Cabin block allowed her to introduce the pale lavenders, peaches, and pinks. The triangles you see are folded fabric pieces (Prairie Points) that have been inserted into the seam. Laurine opted to put a narrow strip of light value fabric between the four G block units, which also helped soften the intensity of the purples.

Laurine's G's , 1998, 54'' x 43''
Laurine Leeke, quilted by Joyce Baromich

Remember that the traditional blocks we are using as frames can be adjusted, in order to make things fit. I find it much easier to design and be creative when I have a place to start. Choosing a block already in existence can be much easier than starting with a piece of plain white paper.

The block frame you choose does not always have to make the block sit straight. There are a number of quilt blocks that would position your initial block on point.

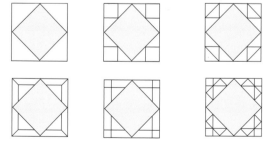

Examples of Framing blocks to position Focus block on point

Delightful, 2000, 64" x 64"
Sharyn Craig

Aunt Sukey's Choice blocks take on a totally different look when set inside a triangle frame.

There was nothing wrong with the original blocks; I just wanted something different, less recognizable as Aunt Sukey's Choice. Even though the blocks were from a friendship group, the size difference was insignificant, so I didn't have to be concerned with that. I did, however, have to unify the blocks color-wise. The framing triangles I added provided me with that opportunity in the quilt named *Delightful*.

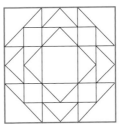

Aunt Sukey's Choice

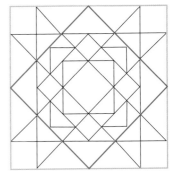

Aunt Sukey's Choice block set inside a pieced triangle frame.

Now, just as you are starting to get comfortable with this concept, here is another one. What if you enlarge a block to be the **set**? Instead of putting one block inside one other block, what if you used each of the squares of a traditional block and filled them with a different block?

Let me explain. This next block is called Best of All or Christmas Star, depending on which book you read. First, you see the original block. Next, I have drawn it with numbers on the plain squares where other Focus blocks might be positioned. The center square could be one larger block, or four smaller blocks.

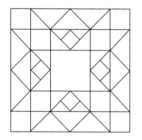

Best of All

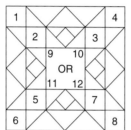

Best of All block. Center could be four small blocks, or one large.

If the original block was 12", then the little squares would be 2" and the center square would be 4". But, if you have 6" Stamp Basket blocks to set and if you use the Best of All block as that setting, then the new "block" would be 36" square. And it only took twelve 6" blocks!

Best of All filled with stars.

Sally Collins, an incredible prize winning small scale quiltmaker and author, agreed to make her interpretation of Best Baskets. Sally's entire quilt is only 13" square. Each basket has a finished size of only 1½".

Bitty Baskets, 1999, 13" x 13"
Sally Collins

My quilt inspired Sally's quilt, but yet a totally unique quilt came out of it. The colors are different, the scale is different, and the border is different. Are you getting the idea?

Best Baskets, 1998, 52" x 52"
Sharyn Craig, quilted by Joanie Keith

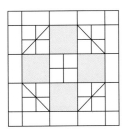

Frame for Crazy Star blocks

Margret Reap had twenty 6" Crazy Stars that she wanted to use to make a relatively large quilt. By doodling on graph paper, she came up with this block to set her stars. Her framing block is 24". Four of these blocks set tangent created a 48" square. Add borders, and pretty soon she had a quilt 72" square—and all from twenty 6" blocks.

Crazy Stars in El Cajon, 1999, 72"x 72"
Margret Reap

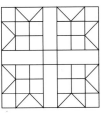

Pink Magnolia block

Pink Magnolia is a Seven-Patch block with lots of squares that could be used for setting other blocks.

Stevii Graves allowed me to work with some 12" Swamp Angel blocks that she had won at a guild. I reconciled the sizes by reducing the blocks to 8" finished size. Using a square up ruler at various skewed angles produced a very liberated set of blocks. In fact, it was Gwen Marston's book, *Liberated Quiltmaking*, that inspired me to do this with the blocks (Refer to page 16 under Twisted Coping Strips to get a feel for how to angle the ruler to create the various effects).

From nine 8" blocks I was able to create a 69" square quilt. This size includes the borders.

You could have used the Pink Magnolia block to set even more blocks. Observe different ways you could have inserted blocks and still have had a balanced quilt.

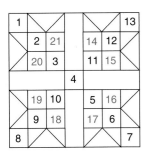

Pink Magnolia block could frame up to 21 blocks

6" blocks = 42" quilt
8" blocks = 56" quilt
12" blocks = 84" quilt

Cheddar Soup, 1999, 69" x 69"
Sharyn Craig, quilted by Lisa Taylor.
Owned by Stevii Graves

You can use this concept of enlarging a block to set your blocks in combination with other setting options. You could sash the portions if so desired or you could use an alternating set of blocks in some of the spaces. You have heard me say this before, but again, "Think outside the box".

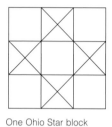

One G block

Margret Reap's thinking led her to include setting G blocks into the four corners of Ohio Star blocks. She then positioned those new blocks inside an Ohio Star block.

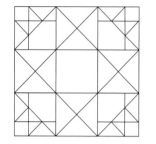

One Ohio Star block

Four G blocks inserted into four corners of the Ohio Star.

Ohio G's, 1998, 39" x 39"
Laurine Leeke, Margret Reap, Carolyn Smith, quilted by Margret Reap

To further inspire you and get your wheels turning, here are a few more block designs that could work when exploring this concept.

The one thing you want to keep in mind with this technique is the size of the initial blocks. Anything much bigger than 8" is going to give you a very large quilt. The blocks don't have to be this small, but be aware of the potential.

Stepping Stone block. Numbered for 28 blocks. (You can place up to 48 blocks.)
6" blocks = 48" quilt
8" blocks = 64" quilt
12" blocks = 96" quilt

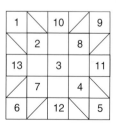

Sister's Choice block. Numbered for 13 blocks. (You can place up to 17 blocks.)
6" blocks = 30" quilt
8" blocks = 40" quilt
12" blocks = 60" quilt

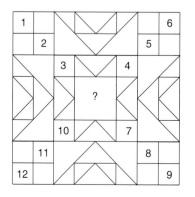

Odd Fellow's Chain block. Numbered for 12-16 depending on center.
6" blocks = 48" quilt
8" blocks = 64" quilt
12" blocks = 96" quilt

CHAPTER SIX

Alternating Possibilities

In the first chapter we defined terms for the basic sets and we identified one of these as the "Alternate set." I stated that the Focus blocks could alternate positions with either a solid square or a secondary pieced block. In this chapter we are going to look more closely at the alternate set and how it can be used as a "solution" with problem blocks.

Here are some things to think about when considering the alternate set:

- It can spice up boring blocks.
- It can calm very busy blocks.
- You can use the alternate block to correct color challenges.
- You can use the alternate block to make a larger quilt from a minimum number of Focus blocks (assuming you don't want to make more of the original blocks.)

Alternate set and alternate blocks are not interchangeable. Alternate blocks and secondary blocks are interchangeable.

Where to Start

First, you have your Focus blocks. Next, you need to decide what block you would like to use for the secondary pattern. The secondary block is frequently a simple block but, if your Focus block is very basic, you might reverse that and select a secondary block that is more complex.

Once you have the two blocks you want to combine, you may find you have to address the issue of how to make the two blocks fit together visually. You may need to adjust the Focus block (coping strips, triangles, or even trimming down), or you could make structural adjustments to the secondary block. You might need to substitute a new shape (design) for a certain portion of the alternating block.

Example: You want to use a simple Nine-Patch block as your connector with an 8" Sawtooth Star block. An 8" Nine-Patch does not result in nice numbers for your pattern pieces.
(8" ÷ 3 = 2⅔") You could either frame the Focus block up to 9" (or even 12") or you could make the adjustment in the secondary block. The resulting connector would look different, but would work the same way.

Instead of the large square in the center of the Four-Patch, you might make smaller squares and create a chain effect. Another possibility for the center might be a Pinwheel block.

Once you have decided which blocks to use, you definitely need to consider how color will work with the design to create the whole. Now is a good time to work on a flannel design wall. Placing your Focus blocks on the wall and auditioning a variety of fabrics for color selection can be really exciting. A set of blocks that is not "working" can quickly become quite intriguing when other colors and fabrics are placed near them.

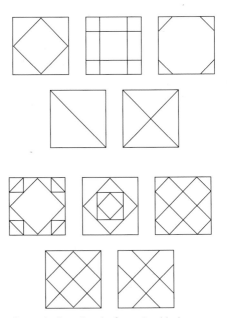

Some simple options for Secondary blocks

 2⅔"
 2⅔"
2⅔"

2
4
2

Nine-Patch block with not so nice numbers

8" Sawtooth Star block

8" Connector block with nice numbers

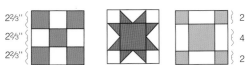

Four-Patch block in center, colored to create a chain effect.

Pinwheel block in center space

Let's look at some quilts. First we have Laurine's *Ohio Star Plus* quilt.

Did you even notice all the blocks were different sizes? In this quilt, all the blocks are derivations of Ohio Star blocks, but imagine using this same set for any assortment of odd-sized blocks you might have lying around.

PROBLEM: Boring blocks of different sizes (one 6", five 7½", and six 9" blocks from a swap.)

GOAL: Make an integrated whole — somewhat larger than the original number of blocks would suggest— Laurine also wanted an "old looking" quilt.

SOLUTION: First she placed coping strips of various accenting colors around all the smaller blocks to bring them up to size. A simple 9" Nine-Patch block was selected for the connector. Note that the light squares in the Nine-Patches are the same fabric as the side and corner setting triangles. This creates the illusion of the dark small squares floating on the surface. Appropriate fabric choices enabled her to create the old-fashioned feel.

Ohio Star Plus, 1998, 48" x 52"
Laurine Leeke, quilted by Joyce Baromich

Double Nine-Patch
block

Stevii Graves decided to adapt the Nine-Patch block into what is called a Double Nine. Instead of a large square in the center and corners, there are little Nine-Patches. Stevii liked the idea of the Nine-Patch and the chain that it could create, but felt that one large simple Nine-Patch would be too bulky for the red-violet swap blocks, and therefore decided on the Double Nine-Patch block.

PROBLEM: Too much red-violet.

GOAL: How to make all those red-violet blocks not seem so red-violet.

SOLUTION: One way to calm down a color is to use its complement. Green is opposite red on the color wheel. Stevii used more of green than she did red-violet. She used the Double Nine-Patch for her connector block. The strong diagonal created by the dark purple little squares creates a diagonal frame around each of the original Focus blocks.

Red-Violet Chain, 1999, 53" x 73"
Stevii Graves, quilted by Lisa Taylor

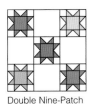

Double Nine-Patch
block with stars

Linda Packer played with the Double Nine-Patch alternating block in a very different way. If you can make a Double Nine-Patch with just squares, why can't you make one with other blocks? The answer is that of course you can. Whether you make small stars, Pinwheels, or whatever, you can position them into the Double Nine-Patch layout.

PROBLEM: Lots of very simple, predictable, identical 9" Ohio Star blocks.

GOAL: Add sparkle and life to the ordinary stars.

SOLUTION: Scrappy stars in similar but different fabrics added the spark that Linda felt was missing in the original blocks. These Ohio Stars are no longer boring, and this is no longer a predictable quilt. How about using your Churn Dash blocks with some miniature Double Nine Churn Dash alternating blocks?

Double Nine/Ohio Stars, 1999, 66" x 66"
Linda Packer

Double Nine-Patch
block made from
Broken Dishes

Laurine used the simple Broken Dishes unit to create a Double Nine-Patch alternating block for her focus blocks.
Very precise use of color created a dynamite setting for the focus blocks. Individually each block was very strong, due to the color. Laurine wanted a way to integrate the various strong blocks into one unified statement.

PROBLEM: Focus blocks that were very strong. The Broken Dishes units were orphans. They had originally been made for another quilt that ended up not happening.

GOAL: Integrate the two projects cohesively into one.

SOLUTION: Use a very precise color placement from the focus blocks in conjunction with the Broken Dishes to frame the original blocks. This allows the eye to rest between blocks and pull the variety of parts together.

Broken Dishes in Color, 1999, 55" x 68"
Laurine Leeke, quilted by Joyce Baromich

Neutral Sampler,
1998, 90" x 66"
Margret Reap,
quilted by Joyce Baromich

Next we have Margret's *Neutral Sampler* quilt. The blocks were from an exchange she had participated in with a group of seventeen friends.

PROBLEM: There were two challenges facing Margret. One, the blocks ranged in size from 6" to 9". And two, how do you set seventeen blocks?

GOAL: Make it all work.

SOLUTION: To solve the size problem, Margret used the coping strip technique. Some of the blocks had plain strips, while others were twisted. Her original blocks were very diverse in size. Once all the blocks were the same size, Margret wanted something just a bit different for the setting. She used a traditional Chimney and Cornerstone Log Cabin and colored in the Courthouse Steps configuration to alternate with the Focus blocks. The darker squares splitting the blocks into four quarters provided the diagonal interest.

Stately Birds,
1999, 90'' x 90''
Margret Reap

For her 50th birthday Margret's friends had given her a collection of 30's reproduction fabrics. She opted to work within that palette for her bird blocks. How could she combine the reproduction, pastel palette with the strong colors of the birds?

This time the chimneys became the lighter value while the Log Cabins were organized to create colored squares around each Focus block. Your eye sees the bird blocks, but it also has plenty of space to rest. Margret could have chosen a very simple sashed set, but that wasn't what she wanted. She wanted something special for the bird blocks. Remember that you can build from something else. You do not have to reinvent the wheel! Remember on page 28, where I dared you to be different? The catalyst came from her *Neutral Sampler* quilt, but Margret worked differently within the framework.

PROBLEM: Margret's mom hand embroidered these state bird blocks and gave them to Margret. The birds were lots of different colors with minor differences in finished sizes. While she loved the blocks, she was concerned about how she could unify them and frame them in a special way.

GOAL: She wanted a way to showcase the blocks and punch them up with color, while not overwhelming the original blocks.

SOLUTION: What if she used the same set as seen on her neutral blocks? Margret began by trimming down the original blocks to be the same size. Four birds were selected to "go together" with sashing. The four bird blocks became the Focus block for this quilt. Rather than treating the birds independently, Margret made a stronger statement by grouping them.

I loved Margret's two quilts and was excited to try the set myself on an entirely different set of blocks. The blocks I chose for the challenge were seven Snow Crystal blocks that my friend Harriet Hargrave had given me.

PROBLEM: How to use seven blocks in varying sizes, each approximately 14".

GOAL: To create a quilt that looked like a contemporary variation of the old-fashioned blocks. The original blocks were primarily red, white, and blue. Since Harriet's quilt had been red, white, and blue when it was finished, I wanted to see if I could make a quilt that wasn't.

SOLUTION: First I picked a palette that emphasized the browns and tans, but ignored the blue. An alternating set, definitely inspired by Margret's two quilts, was chosen. To create another difference in my Log Cabin secondary blocks, I decided to start the Log Cabin block with a 6" LeMoyne Star block. The red chimneys definitely added the diagonal and color interest necessary to keep the viewer's eye moving around the quilt. I found it necessary to first frame each Snow Crystal block with coping strips in order to reconcile the variances in block sizes. Using a dark value fabric as the coping strip allows your eye to focus on the original blocks.

Snow Crystal, 1999, 60" x 94"
Sharyn Craig, quilted by Joanie Keith

Linda Hamby was a participant in the Festival Star exchange.

PROBLEM: Variations in the size of the blocks, plus lack of color cohesiveness.

GOAL: Her goal included making a cheerful, fun quilt for a child's room while resolving size and color issues.

SOLUTION: First, Linda replaced the original triangles in the corners of each Festival Star block with the red fabric. Next, she added a red coping strip to each block before squaring them up to be the same size. A variation of the Chimney and Cornerstone Log Cabin became the alternating pattern for Linda's quilt. She selected some really fun, whimsical novelty prints for the larger center squares of the Log Cabins. She definitely played very successfully with color and pattern when making the alternating blocks. She set her blocks on point with half connector blocks to fill in the edges.

NOTE: These last four quilts shared a common set, but each looks totally different. Spend some time analyzing and comparing for yourself. Now, think about what blocks you might incorporate into this set. What colors would you to use? Would you put your blocks on point to change the feel of the quilt? Instead of the chimney stone effect, could you use triangles?

Festival Star, 1998, 53" x 86"
Linda Hamby

Sage Tracks, 1995,
79" x 100"
Sharyn Craig, quilted
by Lauri Daniells and
Sharyn Craig
Project Map, page 86

PROBLEM: There were two problems I had to address starting this quilt. First was the predictable blocks that ranged from very light to very dark. Second, I wanted to work seventeen blocks into one quilt.

GOAL: To make ordinary blocks into a quilt that would look extremely complicated, but with very simple construction.

SOLUTION: The simple "x" block was chosen for the alternating block. All blocks and framing triangles had to go up on the flannel design wall before I began to sew. Notice how the same exact fabric was used around every single

Sage Tracks block. To construct the quilt, I needed to sew the "x's" one at a time to ensure that each fabric would end up where it needed to be. Half-blocks along the outer edge completed the illusion that the blocks are set on point with diagonal sashing. Check out the Project Map for this quilt on page 86. You will be positively amazed at how incredibly simple it really is. Notice also the insertion of a few little blocks into the border. This is one of those things that takes a little extra time but adds so much to the finished quilt.

Sandy's Sunshine,
1999, 56" x 70"
Sharyn Craig, quilted
by Joanie Keith

Sandy's Sunshine is another guild block-of-the-month set of blocks. Sandy Andersen won them at Sunshine Quilters in 1992. They sat in a closet for seven years until she heard I was looking for problem blocks to play with.

PROBLEM: The blocks were not only uninspiring to Sandy and me, but also very different in size.

GOAL: To make an interesting quilt from predictable blocks.

SOLUTION: These blocks were trimmed down to unify them. During the color auditioning, it was amazing what happened to the predictable little blocks when they were framed with the bright jewel colors. Inspired by the *Sage Tracks* quilt, I felt the challenge was to see what would happen if the "x" was made light instead of dark. I also decided to change the scale of the "x" by re-drawing it on graph paper and making the space for it a much smaller portion of the whole. Using a variety of fabrics for the outer border also added an unexpected finish to the blocks.

The last quilt is called *Night Blooming Peonies*. The peony blocks were made in anticipation of a new workshop I was working on. I had made the blocks myself, so I had only myself to blame for them coming out so much the same.

PROBLEM: These predictable blocks were too much the same.

GOAL: I wanted a set that created a secondary design interest while perking up the blocks.

SOLUTION: The simple square-within-a-square block alternates with the Peony blocks. If you look at the Project Map, page 85, for this quilt you will see how incredibly simple the actual piecing structure is. My use of a strong background fabric that is capable of disguising seam allowances throughout (the black print), also added to the success of this design.

Night Blooming Peonies, 1999, 41" x 41"
Sharyn Craig, quilted by Joanie Keith
Project Map, page 85

Turn to page 24 and look at *Sue's Bees*. This quilt is also an example of an Alternating set. The main alternate block is a very simple square divided in half diagonally then colored half-light and half dark. Now, look at the *Sage Tracks* quilt and *Sandy's Sunshine* quilt on pages 52 and 53. You could modify the connector block used in these two quilts to make it more similar to the one in *Sue's Bees*. The very same thing holds true with the four quilts found in this chapter that use the Log Cabin variation for the alternate block. You do not have to piece all those Log Cabin blocks. You could simply divide your square in half or into fourths and then color those triangles to create similar illusions to the quilts in this chapter.

T
I
P
Think about it. The world of quilts is open to you. It can be exhilarating to realize that you are empowered to make these changes. There are no rules. There is absolutely no reason you have to color within the lines: You are in charge!

CHAPTER SEVEN

Organizing Your Orphan Blocks

An orphan block is one that doesn't seem to belong anywhere. It is just **there**. You don't know what to do with it. It doesn't have to be just a single block; multiples of the same block could be orphans. An orphan might be a leftover from another project, or it could be something you started in a workshop and didn't finish. Perhaps you won block-of-the-month at guild and received five blocks. These orphans can be anything from complex traditional blocks to simple Four-Patches. An orphan could be something quite lovely or pitifully sad. One quilter's orphan might be a treasure to another.

Chances are you have them. Hopefully you haven't thrown them away. Over years of making quilts, these stragglers do keep popping up. I deliberately make extra blocks when working on a quilt in the hope that there will be leftovers. In fact, I have come to think of these little guys as "planned-overs."

Think about cooking a turkey. First comes the big turkey dinner, followed by turkey sandwiches, turkey tetrazzini, turkey salad, and so on. It makes sense to plan ahead this way with cooking, so why not when making quilt blocks?

Keeping track of these leftovers can be quite another matter. Storing leftovers in labeled boxes or bags does make it possible to find them later when you need them. Where to store these boxes and bags? Look in your linen closet. Do you really need all those towels and sheets? Consider how much more practical that same linen closet could become stacked with all your ongoing projects! Closet shelves, under beds, bookcases, dresser drawers—all of these are good candidates for project storage.

Forget the Guilt

While we are on the subject, I really do prefer the term "ongoing" to "unfinished". There is something negative sounding about having unfinished projects.

Guilt is a horrible thing. It troubles many quilters when they have more than two quilts in progress at one time. Forget guilt! Those projects aren't unfinished; they are just "mulling." Like good wine or cheese, they need to age before they are ready. You can't rush the creative process, but, when the mood strikes, you must have your tools handy. By storing any and all ongoing projects in labeled containers, you can easily put your hands on them when you are ready to work with them.

Work With Your Orphans

When we talk about combining various ongoing quilt projects into one quilt, some people jump to the conclusion that what we mean is randomly sewing together a hodgepodge of miscellaneous blocks. If something doesn't fit, you whack it down or slap some strips around it to make it fit. That's certainly one approach, but what I am hoping to expose you to here is a different, more organized approach to working with your orphans.

The quilts you will see on the next few pages are "free" quilts, in the sense that they were made with lots of those miscellaneous odds and ends that we all just seem to have. You might have only a few of one thing but a lot of something else. You could have a lot of Four-Patches because you started them for a project but then didn't like them there, and didn't use them. Now you are stuck with maybe 75 Four-Patch blocks, but this is a bonus, not a mistake!

Mental-health Projects

I have a couple of what I term mental-health projects. One such project is LeMoyne Stars. Another is Half Log Cabin blocks. I work on either of these two projects when I am not currently knee-deep in any other specific project, and absolutely must sew but don't have the energy to be creative. I work on them in the little five and ten minute increments of time that pop up every now and then. Over the period of a year, the number of stars and Log Cabin blocks just keeps growing and growing. When I need some blocks to play with, such as the first time I wanted to play with the Festival Star frame, described on page 35, the blocks are available for that purpose.

But it doesn't matter whether you start now on your own mental health projects or you already have some miscellaneous blocks that you would like to move out of the closet and into a quilt. What is important is that we stop procrastinating and start concentrating on how to organize them into something special.

I suggest you start by finding every single block you own that is not already committed to a specific quilt. This means everything: Log Cabins, Four-Patches, Mariner's Compasses, stars, Rail Fence blocks—everything.

Ways to Group Your Blocks

Next it is fun to sort the blocks into "like" groupings. Now, what comprises a "like" grouping can change from quilter to quilter and from day to day. One way to sort might be by color. Anything that is blue goes in one pile, all the green in another, and so forth. Another way to group your blocks is by pattern. You might put all stars in one pile, baskets in another. Yet another way to separate blocks is by their size. Grouping by a combination of size and color is also a way to put things together. Remember, the size doesn't have to be exact, because we can always fix that, but a 2" Four-Patch block and a 24" Mariner's Compass are probably not going to work together in one quilt (I said "probably". I didn't say it couldn't be done).

Once the sorting is accomplished, decide which pile you would like to play with. If they all look good, flip a coin, but make a selection and see what you have. Once you have a set of blocks you are ready to work with, you are probably going to want to place them on the flannel design wall. You can use the floor, but if they are going to be there for long, a wall is really nice.

Establish a Goal for the Blocks

The next step is pulling fabric to use with the blocks. This can be any fabric, so you need to decide on a direction to go with the blocks. Go back to the adjective game, page 22. Look at the blocks on the wall. What word describes what you are seeing? What adjective do you want to feel? Establish a goal for the blocks. If you know you want to make a quilt for Aunt Elizabeth, whose favorite color is red, that will definitely influence which colors you place on the wall. Pull lots and lots of fabrics. You can always eliminate some later, so begin with more than you can imagine using. Let one color or fabric pull you into the next one. You will find that the more fabric and colors you have out, the more fun this portion of the process becomes.

Getting Started

Now what? You have blocks and you have selected fabric, so what's next? Looking very closely at the quilts on the next pages will hopefully give you a clearer idea of how orphans can work together. Not one of these quilts started out as an idea on paper for which blocks had to be made. All of them were the direct result of blocks hanging around, looking for a place to live. If you like *Starring the Students*, page 64, but don't have a Schoolhouse block, what about that Feathered Star block you made in a workshop? No Log Cabins? No problem! What about all those Split Nine-Patches you have? The idea is to use what you have whenever possible. Sometimes you do have to make a few more of a block to make the quilt work for you, but before you rush to do that, see if you don't have something else that might be substituted.

Joanie's Bits, 1998, 54'' x 54''
Sharyn Craig, quilted
by Joanie Keith

This first quilt is called *Joanie's Bits*. Joanie gave me five Album blocks, five Garden Gal blocks, and four Stars. They weren't color coordinated, they weren't the same pattern, and they definitely weren't the same size.

I fixed the sizes by sewing negative coping strips to each of the Album and star blocks, since the background fabric was still available (I challenge you to find the coping strips). Next the Garden Gal blocks were trimmed down to meet the size of the other blocks (And no, they never had hands. This is the way they came).

Once they were all the same size, the rest was easy. Since the girls were diagonally oriented in the blocks, this became a diagonal quilt. I decided that simple sashing was needed both to separate the blocks and to unify the design. Auditioning many different colors for the sashing resulted in not just one color, but lots of colors. One thing that remains constant throughout is the cheddar fabric used for the cornerstones. You might have made a totally different color choice, perhaps based on a desire to calm down the blocks. I wanted to punch them up. Knowing that goal definitely helped me in the decision making process.

You may not believe this, but all the small triangles used in the side and corner setting triangles were also leftovers. I keep boxes of various sized triangles, mostly so they are available when I want to audition a concept. I use shoeboxes and label them "3'' half-square triangles", and the like. Usually I end up cutting new triangles in a proper color, but the sample triangles help me see what a design might look like. This time I didn't have to cut new triangles, as the scrappy ones were perfect.

Sample This, 1999, 50" x 50"
Laurine Leeke, quilted by Joanie Keith
Owned by Carolyn Smith

Something that can be fun to do is to get together with a group of quilter friends and have everyone bring orphans. I did that with a group of about six other quilters. People shared their blocks, doing a lot of trading, and as a result some really neat quilts were produced.

Carolyn Smith donated three groups of four blocks, each made from a dark purple fabric. Each of the three sets of blocks was a different size. Laurine took the blocks home to play with. She solved the size dilemma three different ways. She cut down the four outer corners. She set together the four little guys in the middle with a strip of light yellow, then put four yellow triangles on the corners. The four Lady of the Lake blocks were okay the way they were. Setting the blocks together in the block framing technique that we learned on page 34 allowed the new fabrics, new colors, and new designs to establish the visual impact necessary to create a quilt that both really like.

Linda's Orphanage, 1999, 66" x 66"
Linda Packer

Linda came with four appliqué blocks. Sandy had the color blocks, and Carolyn volunteered the simple Sawtooth Stars. We placed the blocks strategically on the floor, alternating blocks and color. We were just playing: color wasn't even introduced into the equation at this point. We were just looking for a balance. Linda took the blocks home once we established an idea for layout, and now you can see her result.

The appliqué blocks were cut down to standardize their size. Oversize coping triangles were added to the Star blocks and color blocks before cutting them down to match the size of the appliqué blocks. Careful attention to color placement, combined with the black fabric, makes this quilt so graphic. And just think, it was free! Chances were good that nobody was ever going to do anything with their blocks the way they were. By sharing, Linda got a great quilt and Sandy and Carolyn got rid of some guilt.

Housing Project, 1998, 48" x 66"
Sharyn Craig, quilted by Joanie Keith

Housing Project is the result of six House blocks and four Heart blocks from Sue, six Star blocks from Joanie, and fourteen small Nine-Patches from Stevii. The Nine-Patch blocks went on point, with some red squares and white triangles added to create the connecting chain that holds the houses together. The hearts point in from the corners and the stars fill in the gaps. There were a lot of reds and blues in the houses, hearts, and stars, so staying in that palette provided just a bit of a pick-me-up to the balance and design.

Cosmic Sue, 2000, 47" x 60"
Sally Schneider

Sally Schneider pulled the five Sunbonnet Sue blocks out of a dusty basket to set together with the Log Cabin blocks and small Stars. The Log Cabins and the Sunbonnet Sue blocks could be trimmed to equalize their size with no problem, and the stars were made to fit by positioning some tangent and some with separating strips. Sally did cut and piece the triangle border and strip borders specifically for this quilt. But how much time did that take her? Basically, this is a free quilt.

Something to Crow About, 1997, 56" x 56"
Sharyn Craig

This quilt came together with sixteen approximately 6" Crazy Stars, one bigger-than-12" Crow block, and a bunch of Logs Plus blocks I had made while experimenting. Reconciling the block size by trimming them down to unify solved the size problem for these blocks.

I worked with a very basic, very traditional Log Cabin layout, but instead of all Log Cabin blocks, I used a star in place of an occasional Log Cabin block and the Crow in a place that four Log Cabin blocks could have been. This made a very organized "free" quilt.

If you have been reading and studying the quilts throughout the book, you might already have recognized the purple G blocks in this next quilt by Carolyn Smith. Carolyn, an adult education quilt instructor, is always making samples for her classes. Four of those sample blocks found a new home in the four corners of this quilt. The G blocks filled in the spaces between blocks and she positioned them to make everything else fit together. The four orphan blocks were similar in their coloration to the G blocks. Size-wise they were quite compatible. The G blocks are each 3'', while the class sample blocks are 6''. They didn't start life together, but they sure look good together.

Carolyn's G, 1998, 37'' x 37''
Carolyn Smith

Lynn Kough, also a national quilt teacher, found out about our orphan quilt block party and sent me six blocks that her daughter Katherine had made when she was about ten years old. She placed no restrictions as to what could be done with them, but she hoped that they could get together into a quilt (I suspect she thought she could really stump me with these blocks).

Six blocks is another not-so-easy number to work with. Four of the blocks were red, white, and blue with white backgrounds. One red, white, and blue block had a blue background, and the sixth block was red, white, and black. As might be expected, they were definitely not the same size.

Here I had the problems of size reconciliation, an odd number of blocks to work with, and a bit of a color challenge. Incidentally, have you found the sixth block yet? Look at the north, south, east, and west spaces of the quilt. The sixth block was cut into four quarters. Each quarter of the block was then framed on only two sides to create the square-within-a-square effect you see. The four corner blocks were also framed on only the two outer edges in the same medium blue fabric that became the background for the body of the quilt. The setting gives the blocks a medallion-like effect. The colors blend the sampler blocks together into a unified whole. And, to make things even better, Katherine adores her new quilt.

Katherine's Quilt, 2000, 55''x 55''
Sharyn Craig, quilted by Lynn Kough

Starring the Students, 1990, 64" x 64"
Sharyn Craig

One lonely Schoolhouse block made around 1980, LeMoyne Stars out of that ongoing mental health project box, eight Log Cabin blocks from class sample projects, leftover Four-Patches, one 3" Star block (can you find it?) and somewhere around 500, 2" half-square triangles, left over from a charm quilt made in 1987, provided the resources for this *Starring the Students* quilt. It was all leftovers—orphan blocks that were just lying around.

The sizes were reconciled through a combination of coping strips (the Schoolhouse) and trimming down (the Log Cabin blocks). Spacer borders allowed all the other parts to merge together into this scrappy but cohesive quilt.

I hope these quilts have given you some great ideas about how you can find a solution for your own orphan blocks. You should never be afraid to cut up your blocks, over-dye them, trim them down, add strips to them, or substitute a different block when you don't have the right number. Just because you have nineteen blocks from the friendship exchange does not mean you have to use all of them. If your quilt only needs fifteen blocks, then you have four leftovers for a future project.

CHAPTER EIGHT

Corner Cutters

The quilts in this chapter all have one thing in common: the Corner Cutter technique is used somehow in their creation. A Corner Cutter uses a pattern guide to allow you to easily and simply cut odd shapes. I am going to teach you how to make and use these guides to create odd shapes, such as octagons, trapezoids, and hexagons. Octagons are useful in making the simple Snowball connector block. Trapezoids are found over and over in borders. Hexagons are the foundation of the Sawtooth Star sashing you will see in several of the quilts in this chapter.

We will also look at how you can expand this technique one step further to create secondary designs when setting your blocks together. Check out Linda Packer's *Festival in* G on page 74. You won't believe how incredibly simple it is to achieve that "star block on point" illusion. How about the pinwheels you see at the

corners of the blocks in *Red, Black, and Blue All Over* on page 72? Talk about easy! Yes, it adds a bit more time to the creation of a quilt, but the time is spent in very simple cutting and sewing, which turns into a unique finish.

First we will cover the basic technique. Let's begin by looking at some odd shapes, seen on the bottom of this page.

The math involved in cutting these shapes without a template can be overwhelming, especially if the piece you need is not a "nice" number. Using Corner Cutters gives you a really easy way to cut these shapes without having to make a large template.

First, picture the shape inside a square or rectangle. We are going to create a guide for those little corners, as seen in the illustrations below.

Some odd shapes Corner Cutter technique applies to.

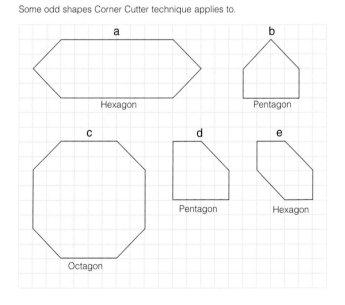

If you were to remove the shaded corners, you would be left with the desired shape.

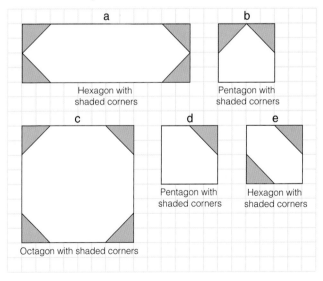

Let's work with a hexagon for our example. We want this hexagon to be 9" finished point to point and 3" finished side to side.

Each of the shaded triangles in our example is a finished 1½" half-square triangle, half of the width of the hexagon shape. You would need a 1½" Corner Cutter guide. The "magic" number you need to remember is ⅛". Your guide is always ⅛" longer than the finished corner size (the corner is the portion you want to eliminate from the square or rectangle that the odd shape fits into).

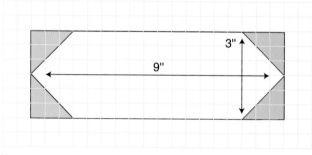

Hexagon

If you want a 2" Corner Cutter, you draw lines 2⅛". To make a 3" Corner Cutter, you draw lines 3⅛".

To create a 1½" Corner Cutter guide, take a piece of 8-to-the-inch graph paper and draw two lines, perpendicular to one another and each 1⅝" long. Connect the ends of the lines. There! You have your guide.

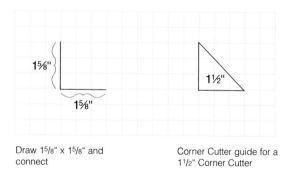

Draw 1⅝" x 1⅝" and connect

Corner Cutter guide for a 1½" Corner Cutter

Once you have created the paper guide, you have two easy options for turning it into a tool to use with your rotary cutter.

Method One

You can secure it to the underneath edge of a rotary ruler, either with tape or glue, with the longest edge of the triangle guide on the edge of the ruler.

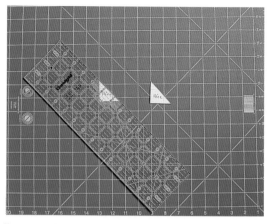

Two options for turning the paper guide into a tool to use with your Rotary cutter.

Method Two

Or you can create a rotary-friendly template by cutting out the paper guide and gluing it to a sturdy template material (my favorite is the John Flynn Cut Your Own Template Kit. If you can't find this laminate material in your local quilt shops, you can order it directly from John Flynn, 1-800-745-3596).

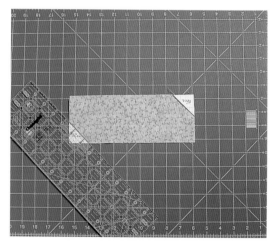

The lower left corner shows how to position the ruler/guide from method 1 to eliminate the corner. The upper right corner shows using the guide from method 2.

Once you have your cutting guide ready, you cut a rectangle (or square, as the case may be) of fabric for the desired shape. You must remember to add seam allowances. In our example, the hexagon is 3" x 9" (finished size). Cut a rectangle 3½" x 9½" and eliminate the corners with the 1½" Corner Cutter. Position the Corner Cutter on the square corners of the shape and trim.

Next, we will do the octagon. The octagon is the mainstay of the simple Snowball block and is used over and over as a connector block. What size is the finished block you want to make? What size are the corners? If you want a finished 6" block with 2" corners, you would cut a 6½" square of the octagon fabric. Next, you would position a 2" Corner Cutter guide on each corner of the square and trim.

How to make the Snowball block

6½" fabric for octagon

Position 2" Corner Cutter
and cut away each corner

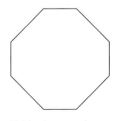

Finished octagon for
Snowball block

Next, you need to cut the replacement triangles. In the previous examples, we assume simple triangle replacements. The "magic" number for cutting these simple half-square triangles is finished size of the triangle plus ⅞". So, if you needed 1½" replacement triangles for the hexagons in our first example, you would cut squares 1½" + ⅞" = 2⅜", then cut once corner to corner. This would give you the exact-sized piece needed to sew onto the hexagon shape.

Cutting replacement triangles

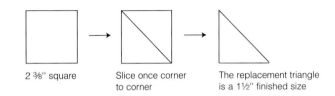

2 ⅜" square   Slice once corner   The replacement triangle
                     to corner   is a 1½" finished size

For the octagon in our snowball example, we need 2" replacement triangles. 2" + ⅞" = 2⅞" square, cut once corner to corner.

> **TIP** *When working with shapes and numbers, it is important that you always talk about the finished sizes of the pieces during the calculation phase, but remember to add the seam allowances before cutting.*

In a Nutshell:

- Corner Cutter guides are always made on 8-to-the-inch graph paper by drawing lines finished size plus ⅛".

- Simple replacement of half-square triangles are always finished size plus ⅞". Cut a square and cut once diagonally.

Let's now look at some quilts that used the technique.

Album, 1998, 56" x 39"
Sharyn Craig, quilted by Joanie Keith

The first quilt you see is this simple *Album* quilt I made. Since I made all the blocks myself, they were fairly uniform in size. I loved the colors, so that wasn't an issue, but I really wanted to keep the blocks simple and understated. An antique quilt inspired the simple diagonal set with Sawtooth Star sashing. The blocks were 8" blocks. My sashing strips were a finished 2½" x 8". I cut muslin strips 3" x 8½" and used a 1¼" Corner Cutter to create the hexagon shape.

Sister's Choice, 1998, 72'' x 72''
Sandy Andersen, quilted by Joanie Keith

Sandy Andersen set her *Sister's Choice* friendship blocks with the same Sawtooth Star sashing. When the cornerstones are light, instead of dark like the points, a totally different effect results. Now, instead of looking like the Sawtooth Star sashing, it appears like a triangle frame to the original blocks. The color challenge with these blocks was really a difficult one, but one would never suspect that looking at Sandy's quilt (look at my quilt made from the same blocks on page 39—it will blow your mind).

Album Optional, 1999, 72" x 72"
Sharyn Craig

In *Album Optional* I played with the same exact setting but looked for a way to make it appear different. What if I didn't eliminate all the corners? What if there wasn't a star at every intersection? Look carefully. There are only four whole stars, some plain squares, and the arrow shapes around the outer edge. I auditioned red triangles (from one of my orphan boxes) on the wall until I was satisfied with the design. I then knew exactly how many of each shape I needed.

I also used the Corner Cutter technique when cutting the setting triangles for this quilt. I drew the setting triangle to scale on a piece of graph paper to begin with. What do you know about this side setting triangle? You know that the blocks were 9" finished. You know that the sashing is 2½". That means that the side setting triangle is 11½" on each short side. I took a large sheet of graph paper and drew two lines 11½" x 11½", perpendicular to one another. I then connected those two lines to create a triangle. You may have to tape several sheets of graph

paper together if you don't have large enough pieces. I measured 3" from the hypotenuse of the triangle and drew a line parallel to that edge. I next measured another 1½" and drew a second line. By making these distances "nice" numbers, I could work with the corresponding Corner Cutters to create the trapezoid shapes I needed.

Drawing the Setting Triangle

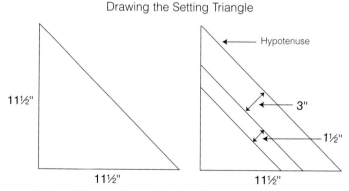

Measure 3" from hypotenuse, then draw line.
Measure over 1½" from that line and draw second line.

Let's create secondary designs at block intersections using the Corner Cutter technique. Each of these next three quilts showcases the results of that very technique. A plain corner is eliminated and replaced with a more involved pieced design. If you do that to each of four blocks, when they are sewn back together the secondary design occurs.

We are going to begin by assuming that you need to frame your blocks first. You can frame with either plain strips or triangles.

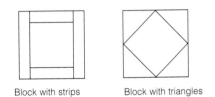

Block with strips   Block with triangles

The size of the strips or triangles will decide the size of the corners. For our example, let's sew 3" strips to 9" blocks. Be sure to iron and trim the block if needed to make it even and tidy around the edges. This is a great opportunity to reconcile size if you need it.

Let us assume for our example that we want 3" corners. We need a 3" Corner Cutter (remember, if you are making it from scratch, it will measure 3⅛" on each short leg). Position the Corner Cutter and trim the corners from the framed block.

Trimming corners from framed block

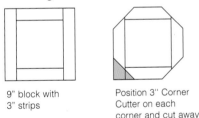

9" block with   Position 3" Corner
3" strips   Cutter on each
                       corner and cut away

Next, determine the design for the replacement triangles. This time we are not going to sew plain 3" triangles back on, but instead a patterned or pieced triangle. You can play on graph paper, or use one of the designs shown at the right. If you work on graph paper, start by drawing two lines, each 6" long and perpendicular to each other.

Connect the tips of the lines to form a square.

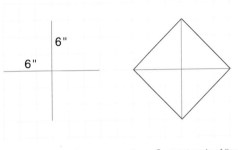

6" lines perpendicular to one another   Connect ends of lines

I let my eye follow the lines of the graph paper to see what designs I can come up with. You will only be working with one fourth of the design during the actual sewing, but by designing the whole, you can see what they would look like when sewn together. It will be simple straight line seaming when you sew the triangle pieces together first, then attach to the corner of the original block. When four blocks intersect you have the pattern.

Star pattern as one
possibility for
corner design

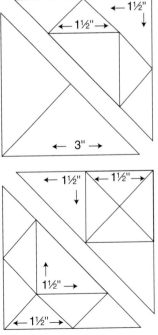
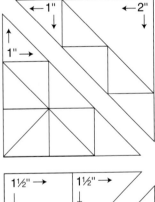
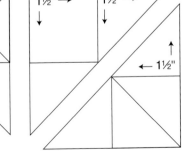

Some possible corner set triangle designs. These are finished size, not rotary cutting numbers.

Red, Black, and Blue all Over, 1999, 45" x 45"
Sharyn Craig

The *Red, Black, and Blue All Over* quilt might as well have been in Chapter 7, *Organizing Your Orphan Blocks.* I had three of one pattern, three of another, two of a third design, and one more lonely star. The one lonely star is the only block that has any black in it. The other eight blocks are primarily blue and purple, yet the quilt reads as black, gray and red. Two of the blocks were 7½"; the other seven were 8". By framing the blocks with strips of either black or gray, I was able to equalize the sizes easily. Yes, they are coping strips! Maybe this quilt should have been in chapter 2 on *Reconciling Size Differences.* I had problems of color, size, and odd numbers of blocks, yet what I created is a blended whole. The corners were pieced to form pinwheels only at the four inside spots. Matching their colors with the framing pieces made it difficult to see the piecing structure. I had auditioned pinwheels at every corner (sixteen total), but it was too much on this quilt. Instead of doing nothing around the outside, I elected to sew plain red triangles back on, giving the outer edge that interesting shape.

Better Cheddar, 1999, 60'' x 60''
Sharyn Craig. Owned by Stevii Graves

Better Cheddar and Festival in G, page 74, work great with pattern blocks at all intersections. You might recognize these Swamp Angel blocks in *Better Cheddar* (on page 43, check out *Cheddar Soup*). These are two totally different solutions using the same exact blocks. It is okay to make more than one quilt from blocks you have. Just because you have twenty-four blocks does not mean they all have to go together into one quilt!

Festival in G, 1997, 64″ x 64″
Linda Packer

Linda Packer made *Festival in* G. Linda is definitely not a purple person. So, when she heard me say: "If you don't like the original colors of the blocks don't put any more of those colors in the quilt," she decided to approach the blocks that way. "No more purple!" became her motto.

Linda also felt that the blocks lacked unity of design, so to create a stronger pattern for the viewer's eye she set her purple blocks inside the Festival Star block. Her next decision was to frame every other block with the pink fabric and the alternate blocks with the green. Linda's quilts frequently take on the feel of an antique quilt no matter how the blocks start out, so this particular pink and green combination was a very natural choice for her.

The mustard yellow for the corner stars is also a reproduction fabric. When you look at this quilt you notice the pink and green, and probably the mustard

color next. Would you ever see the purple if I hadn't told you it was there? She resolved color and size, and created a unique quilt.

You have seen three very similar quilts here, yet no two have the same blocks. No two are the same colors. No two have the same design unit at the corners. Each is different. Each quilt is unique. That is what I want for you. You can now use these quilts as they were intended: as visual stimulation. How might you use what you have learned here to solve problems with a set of your own blocks? Have you thought about the prospect of putting the framed blocks on point? I wonder what that would look like! What if you set the framed blocks with sashing? That would give you another place to play with design. Could we perhaps play with the Sawtooth Star sashing at the same time as the Corner Cutter with secondary design exercisse?

As we get ready to end this chapter, I thought you might enjoy seeing the design evolution process. My first step is always to place the blocks on the flannel wall in a straight set orientation, exposing the flannel wall in an increment that might be equal to sashing.

Next begins the fabric audition process. My automatic response to the blocks is to add more blue. I made no attempt to make the fabric pieces neat and tidy on the wall. They are just randomly scattered around the blocks.

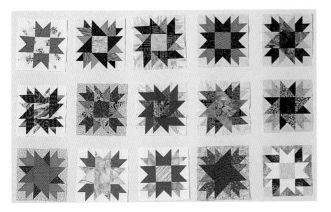

Plain Blue Blocks

Auditioning blue fabric with the blocks

Next, I decided to see what it would look like if I added some green to the wall.

And maybe an accent of yellow?

Green fabrics get randomly positioned with the blues.

Auditioning yellow fabric along side the blues and greens.

Once I had a color palette to work with, my next step was deciding how to use the fabrics. In this case, I decided to add coping strips and coping triangles to the blocks. One block would have blue strips and green triangles; the next would be green strips and blue triangles. I introduced more intense blues and lots of greens. This gave me the opportunity to reconcile size and correct color. I added lots more blue and green fabric than I had originally auditioned. Sometimes during auditioning I position a fabric that doesn't make the final cut. At the early stages, it is important that you don't jump to hasty decisions or feel the need to know everything. Start with an idea, a concept, or a feel for the color, and go from there.

I knew the yellow needed to be the spark, so I had deliberately avoided it in the initial framing. The next step, after framing the blocks was to audition yellow corner triangles in several different ways.

Then I thought about sashing and yellow corners. If I move the blocks apart on the wall, representing sashing, and position yellow triangles on the corners, I get an illusion of the Shoofly block—especially with a yellow corner stone.

I liked the sashing and I liked the yellow, but I decided that the plain triangles were not interesting enough for the rest of the quilt. Doodling on graph paper produced a design I liked, So I tried the new design on the blocks.

Plain framed blocks

A Pinwheel shape can be created with four simple yellow triangles.

An illusion of the Shoofly block

Light sashing with yellow pieced triangles

I liked the blocks and I liked the design, but I came to the conclusion that, for my taste, the quilt was now getting too light. What if I used some blue sashing? I liked the blue I auditioned, but I didn't have enough of it, so it was time to go shopping. Remember that auditioning doesn't always have to be done with the actual fabrics you will be using. Using fabrics close to the same color and value is what's important, not the actual fabric.

I have another idea. If I eliminate the corners from the blue sashing pieces and sew yellow triangles back on,

I will get yellow stars at the intersections. Let's see how it looks.

Some people work and design on graph paper. Some quilters love playing with computer quilting design programs. Me? I love to play with fabric. I love to see, touch, and feel my design. You may find a different process that works best for you, but if you have never tried designing directly with fabric, you definitely need to consider it.

Blue sashing with yellow pieced triangles

Stars

Construction was accomplished with the Corner Cutter Technique. I eliminated the four corners of the framed block with a 3½'' Corner Cutter

I next sewed the replacement triangles and attached them to the block.

The evolution of a quilt is an ongoing challenge and process. This quilt took me months to fully resolve. I liked several of the designs that I had auditioned, but not well enough to sew them together. If you don't feel right about what you see, you need to wait until it does feel right. The longer you quilt, the more you will be able to tell whether you are avoiding making the decision because of fear or because it isn't right. I have learned so much from my mistakes. I have always felt it better to make a decision and move on than to never follow through with what I am working on, and have always figured that even the wrong decisions are better than no decisions.

Eliminating corners from framed block using corner cutter guide.

Replacement triangles attached to block .

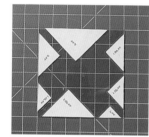

Corner Cutter ruler

BONUS: Here are some full-sized Corner Cutter Guides for you to use. If you would rather use mine than your own, you may photocopy them at 100%.

Why not make yourself a permanent Corner Cutter ruler with a variety of the guides permanently positioned? You can purchase a piece of plain plastic at a picture framing store or plastics supply house (a 6'' square is a nice size). Position the guides with glue or tape and, for even more protection, cover the guides with clear Contact® paper.

Bonus Corner Cutting Guides

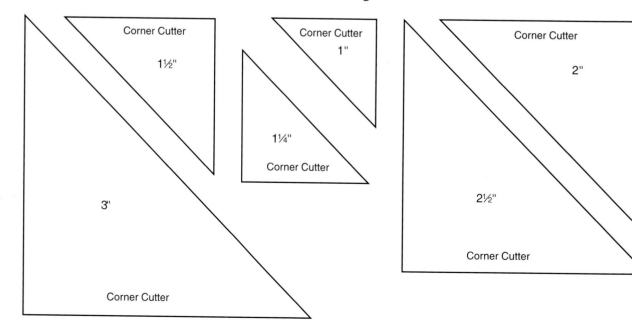

Corner Cutter

1½''

3''

Corner Cutter

Corner Cutter

1''

1¼''

Corner Cutter

Corner Cutter

2''

2½''

Corner Cutter

Starring the Blues, 2000, 80'' x 90''
Sharyn Craig, quilted by Joanie Keith

CHAPTER NINE

Project Maps

In this chapter, I want to provide you with some simple blueprint-like drawings that feature some of the quilts from the book. By reducing a quilt to the block and grid structure and removing the coloration and fabric choices, these drawings really reduce the mystery of construction. Many of the quilts in the book look really difficult but are actually incredibly simple. The maps themselves look very uninteresting. I deliberately did not draw in the Focus blocks, so you will know where to position your blocks. As much as possible, I have tried to present the Project Maps so that the Focus blocks are a 1" square. That will allow those of you who want to play on paper first to draw your block on graph paper to a finished 1", then photocopy, cut, and paste as much as necessary. Some of the maps are of the entire quilt, including a border, if one was needed to illustrate part of the piecing structure. One map is only for the border design. I cannot tell you how many times I get asked about the border on my *Festival Star* quilt, page 35. It really isn't a difficult border to piece. I do graph it out on paper, and I make templates. Using the John Flynn template material allows me to successfully rotary cut without destroying the template—See the information on page 66. Many people think that this is a quick strip pieced border. Sorry, but it isn't. Making the border does add a bit more time to the creation of the quilt, but it isn't that much extra time, and I love the way it uses so many different fabrics and colors. I also enjoy playing around with how it is broken down and colored. The border on *Something to Crow About* (page 62) is a variation of this same border. You can read more about this border on page 88, where it is discussed in detail.

Some of the Project Maps are what I will term Mini Maps. I haven't drawn the whole quilt, only enough to show you the structure. Other times, I have included the whole quilt. Do not think that you have to use the exact number of blocks illustrated on any particular drawing. You certainly can add or subtract rows as necessary.

Feel free to change orientation of any of these maps. If I use straight set blocks on a particular map, what would happen if you put them on point? If a map shows tangent blocks, ask yourself what they would look like with sashing. If you decide to do sashing, should it be light or dark? Should you use simple, plain strips, or more involved piecing?

Is there a way you could combine what you have learned from the chapter on Corner Cutters to create a quilt that could fit into one of these Project Maps? The more you know, the more you can change. I want you to learn to become independent!

I have drawn the Project Maps with very light graph paper lines in the background so you can truly see what size a piece needs to be. Assign a unit of measure to each graph paper square: (such as 1" or 1½") If you don't like the number you come up with as it relates to your Focus blocks, consider using coping strips around the blocks first.

As I told you before, I don't design on graph paper first. I design on the flannel wall with my blocks and fabric. I audition and play. Sometimes, in order to figure out how to piece something I have created on the wall, I do get out graph paper and doodle. My drawings are definitely not fancy when I do this. See for yourself in the photo, on the next page, of my actual doodling for my *Festival Chain* quilt. I am going to give you a Project Map for this quilt, but do take note of the skimpiness of the design that I worked with.

I hope the Project Maps will help you take one more step towards getting your problem blocks resolved. Once you see how simple these maps are, perhaps you will attempt to analyze other quilts that you see and find their simple piecing structure. Remember, though, I am daring you to do something different with your quilts. You can follow the exact grid, but because you don't have the same blocks in the same colors, your quilts will look different. If you have LeMoyne Star blocks, choose a setting besides one of the ones shown with LeMoyne Stars. After all, you know what that will look like. What would LeMoyne Stars look like in the Map for *Margret's Basket* quilt, on page 38?

Working graph paper doodle for *Festival Chain*

Suggestions *for* How to Use the Project Maps

- Draw your own Focus blocks on graph paper to be scaled at 1". Photocopy, then cut and paste to play with design.

- Assign a unit of measurement to the graph paper grid you see behind the maps (drawn in blue).

Example: 1 square = 1", or 1 square = ½", or 1 square = 3". If there are 4 graph paper grids across and your unit of measurement is 1" per grid, the space would be equal to 4".

You can assign any unit of measurement that you wish.

- Feel free to photocopy and color the maps to create designs.

- All maps can be adjusted to accommodate different numbers of Focus blocks.

Project Maps

Festival Chain

The quilt can be seen on page 18.

What if you didn't use the alternating chain block, but instead used more Focus blocks?
How about setting the original blocks straight rather than on point?

The Trouble With Purple

The quilt can be seen on page 18.

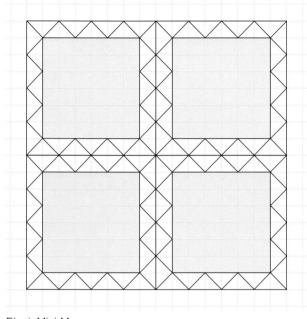

Blank Mini Map

Colored Mini Map to show my interpretation

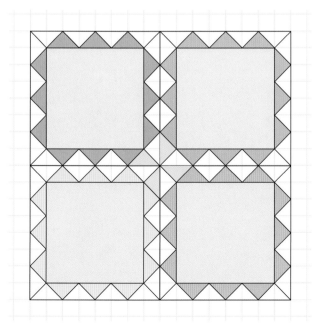

What if colored different?

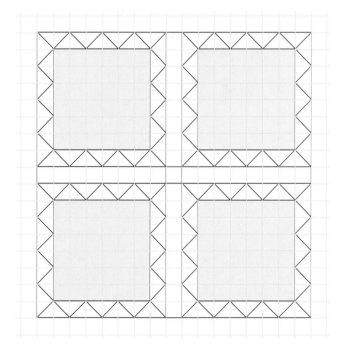

What if separated by sashing?

It Takes a Village/Autumn Splendor

The quilts can be seen on page 32.

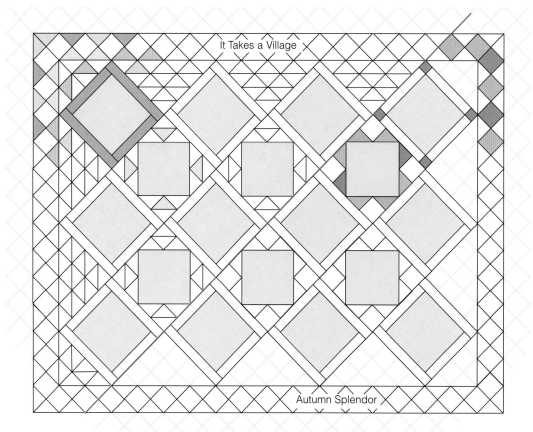

By changing the piecing structure slightly in both the coping triangles and strips, you are able to introduce different design elements into the equation. Play with coloration on this setting. Study the other quilts in chapter 4 to see how you can modify this Project Map to accommodate one of the other designs. The *Autumn Splendor* border in the diagram is slightly modified from the quilt on page 32.

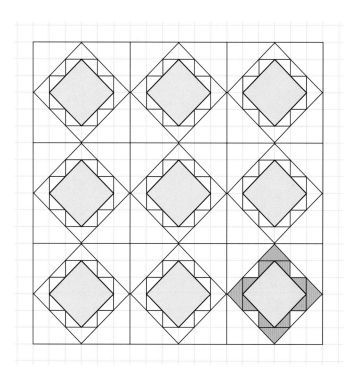

Margret's Basket

The quilt can be seen on page 38.

Only one block is colored in, so that you can relate to the original quilt. What other designs can you create by coloring differently?

Windy Stars/For My Baby

The quilts can be seen on page 37.

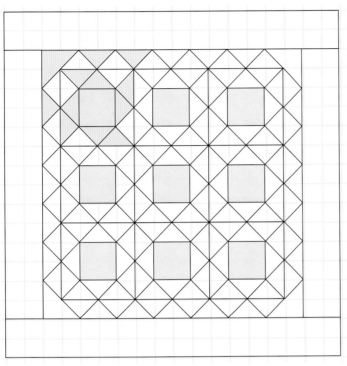

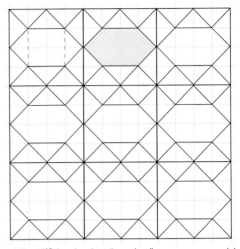

What if? Look what "erasing" one seam could do to the entire design. You could still create a quilt with Focus blocks and seams. But change value/color position to trick the viewer's eye.

Food for thought. What if you introduced sashing into the set? Or put the blocks on point instead of straight?

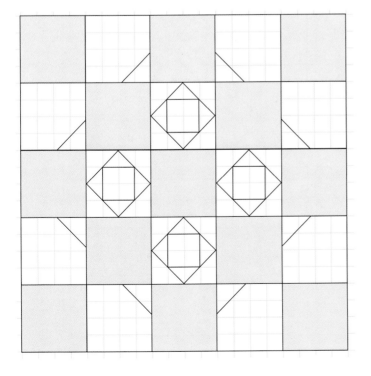

Night Blooming Peonies

The quilt can be seen on page 54.

This particular Project Map doesn't look interesting by itself, but look at the original quilt and you will see why this one had to be included. Careful fabric selection contributed to the illusion of difficulty in the original quilt. Keep this in mind as you select fabric for your quilts. I used two different connector blocks in the creation of this quilt, but what if you used all the same ones? How else could they be colored? Could you put the Focus blocks on point?

Sage Tracks

The quilt can be seen on page 52.

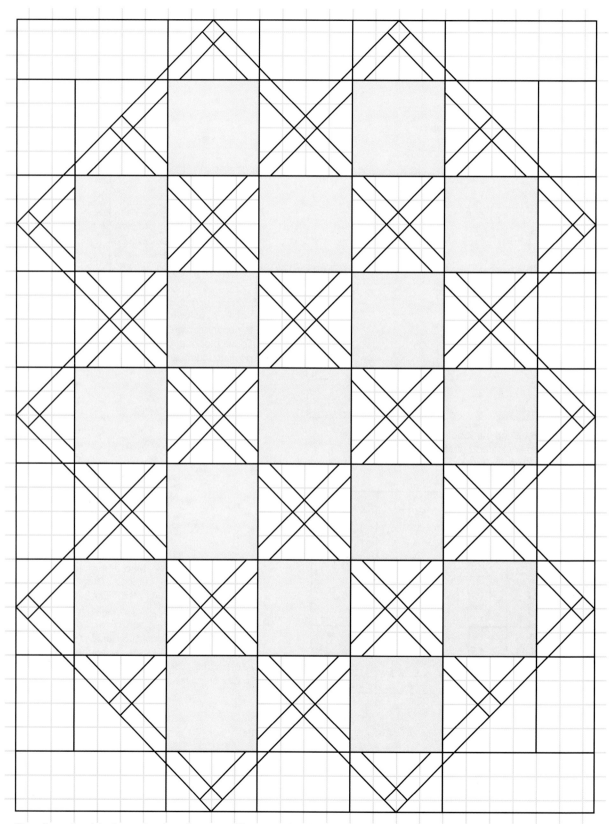

The alternating block can be done in many different scales. Look back at the original quilt, page 53 then at *Sandy's Sunshine,* page 53. You will notice that they are basically the same alternating block with different divisions and the playful use of color to create a secondary design.

Starring the Blues

The quilt can be seen on page 79.

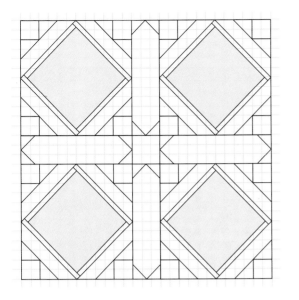

When color is removed from the equation, the design shows up much better. Remembering that the original quilt was in the Corner Cutter chapter should tell you that you are free to alter the corner replacement triangle design. Come up with a totally different design! Look at the step-by-step photos in that chapter and notice how easy it would be to work with this map but totally change the outcome.

Playful Garden

The quilt can be seen on page 20.

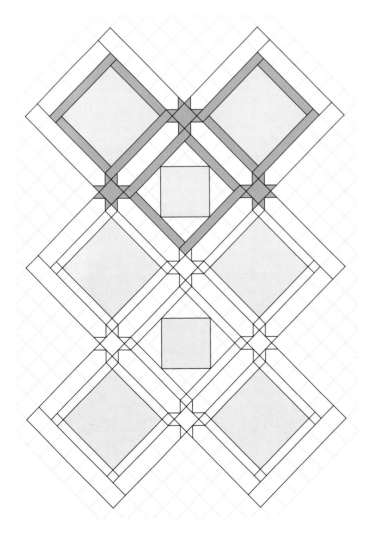

The original quilt had two blocks, of distinctly different sizes, but yours certainly don't have to be that way. Your blocks could all be the same and you can still use the framework of this set. Construct this set by framing the focus blocks with strips of, in this case, green fabric, squared up then set with sashing and corner stones. The shaded triangles are colored to match the corner stones, which is why you achieve the garden maze latticework effect.

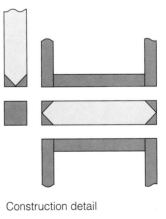

Construction detail

Sharyn's *Festival Star/Something to Crow About*

Quilts can be seen on pages 35 and 62.

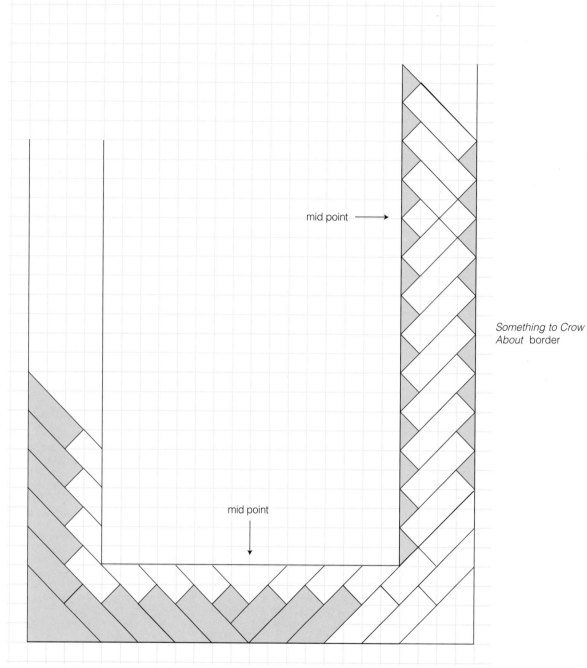

mid point →

mid point ↓

Something to Crow About border

Festival Star border

Every time I show my quilts *Festival Star* and *Something to Crow About*, someone asks about the border design. For that reason, I am including the map and suggested design ideas for these two borders and showing how they can be modified to accommodate your quilt.

This border is amazingly versatile. It is a terrific way to use lots of different fabrics, which makes it particularly effective on a scrappy quilt. I have always found it necessary to draw this border (scaled down) on graph paper first. It can be any width and any coloration, and use any division of space (as you'll see in the illustrations). Here are some guidelines that I have found to be helpful. Remember, these are guidelines, not rules.

- Use an even number of units and reverse the design in the center.

- When drawing the design on graph paper, I begin by drawing a square, or at least 2 edges of the **quilt** equal to the size of the original quilt. (1 graph paper square = 1'') I then decide how much total width I want the border to add to the quilt. If it is 6'', I draw a second square, 6 graph paper lines away from the first square.

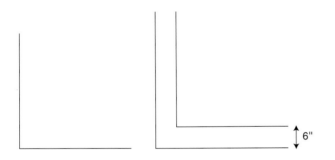

- Starting in a corner, the next reference point is also 6'' away, if I am adding 6'' (up and over 6 graph paper lines, connect the corner to this new reference point).

If the width of the border design segment is 3'', I next draw those pieces in, each 3 graph paper lines apart.

- Divide the slices at any point you wish. I recommend that you keep square corners by following graph paper grids.

You definitely want to play with coloration. Should the inside pieces or the outside pieces use the light value?

- I make templates using the John Flynn template material (see page 66). This material is incredibly easy to cut and totally rotary friendly.

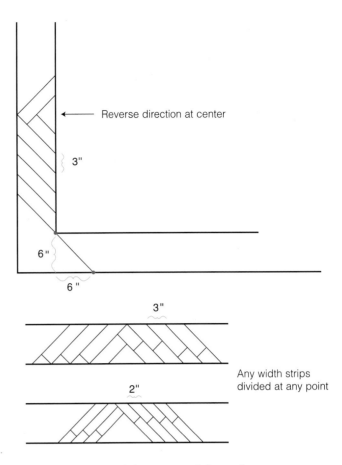

- Keep in mind that many of these designs are directional. As such, it will be important that you cut both right-facing and left-facing units in order to create the design.

- If you find that the size of your original quilt doesn't work easily with the number or size of the units you draw, it is possible to add border frames (coping?) to the quilt first, making the quilt come out a nice size (Don't forget seam allowances!).

In a Nutshell:

As with everything in this book, use the information, inspiration, and ideas to jump-start your own creative juices. Pull elements from many different quilts to solve the problems with your blocks. When you read a detective novel, don't you find yourself trying to figure out the answer before the author reveals it to you? Well, in a way, our blocks are a part of a detective story too. I have given you lots of clues, hints, and ideas, but now I want you to solve the problem and come up with your own solution. And remember you gain confidence through experience. Each quilt you make is a new challenge, a new set of problems, and a new solution. Relax and enjoy!

CHAPTER TEN

Wrap it Up

In this final chapter I would like to do two things. First I would like to talk about friendship block exchanges, since so many of the quilts in this book are the direct result of these swaps. Second I would like to create a cross-reference to some of the quilts in the book. The cross-reference will include quilts that share a setting, as well as quilts that contain the same blocks. Due to the subject structure of this book, it was impossible to have all the like-block quilts together in one place. But it is going to be fun for you to see how different the quilts can actually look when colors are totally different and set structure changes.

Exchanges

In 1992, I joined a group of sixteen quilters whose purpose was to make blocks to trade with one another. We met three to four times a year. We would decide on our block assignment as a group, and when we got together the next time we were each to have made sixteen blocks, fifteen that we would then trade with one another, one of our own to keep.

Some of you are undoubtedly wondering why. Why would I willingly do this, when we all know that the blocks would never be the same size, and I wouldn't like all the color choices the different quiltmakers have made? Isn't it easier to make your own blocks, blocks that you know you are going to like in the end? Isn't it easier to cut and sew all your own blocks so you can be in control of the quality? The answer is of course it is. But, you know what? It isn't as much fun. My blocks are predictable. My blocks have no soul. My blocks don't remind me of the fun I have had with all these quilters I have come to call my friends.

The quilts I have made since 1992 are some of the best I have ever made. I have been challenged in ways I never would have been if I had made all my own blocks. I have enjoyed this experience so much that in 1994, I started a second group that would also exchange blocks. The structure of the two groups is a bit different. I will share the differences with you, so that you might get the courage to form such a group for yourself and your quilter friends. You can borrow ideas from any I share or make up your own rules.

In Group 1, the group decides the assignment. In Group 2, I decide the assignment. Group 1 meets three or four times a year. Group 2 meets only twice a year. In the spring, I give out the assignment to all participants in Group 2. In the fall, we meet to trade blocks. In the spring, when Group 2 gets together again, they must have a quilt top together from the blocks they got in the fall. In Group 2, it is not an option to not make a quilt top. Group 1 has no such stipulation. There are benefits to both ways here, so don't be too hasty to jump to one conclusion over another. In Group 2 we quickly see how totally different the same blocks look when colored and set differently. In Group 1, some of the members never set any of their blocks together. This group likes not having the pressure of having to perform. Many of the members have been quite content to just make and collect blocks. Most people in the group, however, have put at least half of the blocks together.

Certain assignments in each group incorporated some color lessons or piecing challenges. A color lesson might involve creating a transparency, or it could be to work only in monochromatic, or adjacent, or complementary color schemes. A piecing challenge might have been to design a center for a block frame (like the *Festival Star* block you read about in Chapter 5).

I am going to outline a few of the challenges that have been tackled and include diagrams of the particular block that we used, when appropriate. I do want to mention that, for the most part, we have not known the name of the original block as we were working. That was very deliberate. If you know the name of the block, you are influenced by the way you think it should look. If you have no preconceived idea of what a block is supposed to look like, you definitely tend to be more creative. I am not including the names here, with very few exceptions, for the same reason. I am not trying to deny credit or claim it for myself. I did not invent any of these blocks. Sometimes a block we used was one seen in an old *Country Living* magazine or in an ad that came in a mailer. We truly did not know the name or source of the original block. There were times that a number of block line drawings were presented to the group to vote on. In those situations the blocks were named "A", "B", "C", and so on. When you see the "G" block challenge, now you will know why it is called that.

There were never any restrictions placed on the quiltmakers as to how to set their blocks, how many of the blocks they received that they had to use, or what colors they could use in the setting. Once the blocks were the property of any one person, they could do whatever they wanted (that included sharing them with one another. Occasionally someone would make a quilt that didn't use all the blocks, and discover someone else had designed a quilt that needed a few more. We were free to give blocks to other people).

I hope you will feel free to use any of these challenges or create your own. You will learn so much from the opportunity. It will be hard, but it will also be incredibly rewarding. I would like to make two suggestions if you do decide to start a group of your own. First, I would suggest a maximum of twelve people. More than twelve people can lead to some really big quilts. Also, when you meet in homes, as we do, it is often hard to fit more than twelve people. Secondly, keep the size of your blocks reasonable, preferably under 10'', unless the block has an awful lot of pieces or is very difficult to piece. Smaller blocks have more setting solutions that don't compromise integrity of the design.

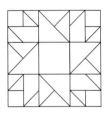

Blue block

Blue Blocks

The assignment here was to work only in blue, any shade, tint, and value. We could include neutrals, such as white and off-white. We were playing with the monochromatic color scheme. After we had the blocks, we could incorporate any color we wanted into the setting of the blocks.

QUILTS:

It Takes a Village, page 32

Starring the Blues, page 79

Red, Black, and Blue All Over, page 72

Iced Stars, page 26

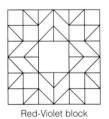

Red-Violet block

Red-Violet Blocks

Group 2 voted on which of a number of blocks they wanted to use, and we selected block F. Each person purchased approximately one yard of the same red-violet fabric that I had pre-determined and had on hold at a local quilt shop. That fabric had to appear in at least one piece on each block. Any other color could be used with the red-violet in their blocks.

QUILTS:

The Trouble With Purple, page 18

Coloring for Fun, page 27

Simple Gifts, page 31

Red-Violet Chain, page 46

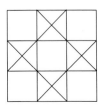

Basic Ohio Star block

Ohio Star Plus

We were to each use the basic Ohio Star block, but to plug some other pieced structure into the four corners of the block. We could make our blocks either 6'', 7½'', or 9'' finished size. The color assignment was "plaid."

QUILTS:

Ohio Star Plus, page 19

Ohio Star Plus, page 46

Ohio Stars and More, page 30

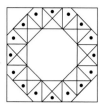

Festival Star block

Festival Star Blocks

You are going to see two different kinds of quilts that fall into this category. Some quilts were from the basic assignment, but others used the Festival Star frame, as described in Chapter 5, to set their own blocks. Both kinds of quilts will be listed in the reference section. The quilts with the * mark are the ones from the original exchange. The assignment was to replace the octagon (or square) in the center of the block with something of interest. That interest could be a pre-printed motif, but it could not be an all-over, non-descript patterned fabric. It could be pieced, appliqué, stitchery, and so on. All blocks were 11" finished and each person was to use a neutral light in the same position (noted by the •).

QUILTS:
Nancy's Festival Star*, page 36
Festival Chain*, page 18
Festival in G, page 74
Sharyn's Festival Star, page 35
Festival Star*, page 51

G block

G Blocks

This time, our blocks were 3" finished size. Each person was to make four identical G blocks for everyone. They were to put the four identical G units in a zippered baggie and bring them to the exchange. We each had to use purple and could only use the colors adjacent to purple on the color wheel—(in other words, from blue to red) You had to use purple. You did not have to use both red and blue, but you could have.

These blocks were specifically selected because they were asymmetrical. People's independent choices for setting their blocks together created some really different quilts. Any colors could be used when it was time to set the blocks together.

QUILTS:
Festival in G, page 74
Carolyn's G's, page 63
Laurine's G's, page 40

Block used for
color wheel study

Color Wheel Study Blocks

There were thirteen people in this exchange. The names of thirteen colors (including black) were written on separate slips of paper, folded, and placed in a paper bag. The bag was passed around and we each picked one out. You were to color the block with a black square in the center, then move from the darkest to the lightest shade of your color. The lightest shade of your color was to be the background; you could use no other neutrals. You were to use prints, as opposed to the hand-dyed solids.

QUILTS:
Linda's Orphanage, page 59
Broken Dishes in Color, page 47

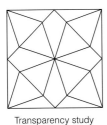

Transparency study

Transparency Study Blocks

We were exploring how to create a transparency. Some of us succeeded and some of us didn't, but the point is that we tried. We each had to use red somehow in our blocks and neutral light in the same background position.

QUILTS:

Light Show, page 30

Barbara's Transparencies, page 33

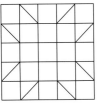

Sister's Choice

Sister's Choice Blocks

We were each given a 3" square cut from the same floral print fabric. We could use only the colors found in our swatch. We had to use at least one piece of black in the blocks.

QUILTS:

Sister's Star, page 39

Sister's Choice, page 69

The Trouble with Purple, page 18

Other quilts to cross-reference and compare throughout the book include:

Swamp Angel Blocks

Cheddar Soup, page 43

Better Cheddar, page 73

LeMoyne Stars Blocks

Sharyn's Festival Star, page 35

Windy Stars, page 37

Starring the Students, page 64

Crazy Stars Blocks

Crazy Stars in El Cajon, page 43

Something to Crow About, page 62

Same Star Blocks

Asilomar Logs, page 17

Ripley Star, page 31

Star of the Lake, page 38

Red, Black, and Blue all Over, page 72

Same Sashing Blocks

Tea Basket Challenge, page 14

Festival Chain, page 18

2-for-1 Set Blocks

Ohio Stars and More, page 30

Light Show, page 30

Simple Gifts, page 31

It Takes a Village, page 32

Autumn Splendor, page 32

Ripley Star, page 31

Barbara's Transparencies, page 33

Katherine's Quilt, page 63

Same Alternating Set Blocks

Sandy's Sunshine, page 53

Sage Tracks, page 52

Same Alternating Set with Log Cabin Variation Blocks

Snow Crystal, page 50

Neutral Sampler, page 48

Stately Birds, page 49

Festival Star, page 51

Same Alternating Set with Double Nine Variations Blocks

Red-Violet Chain, page 46

Double Nine/Ohio Stars, page 47

Broken Dishes in Color, page 47

Same Set: Framed and C.C./Secondary Design Blocks

Red, Black, and Blue all Over, page 72

Better Cheddar, page 73

Festival in G, page 74

Twist 'n Turn Variations Blocks

Asilomar Logs, page 17

Celebration, page 19

Joanie's Patriotic, page 27

Saturday Night Live, page 7

Sawtooth Star Sash Blocks

Playful Garden, page 20

Sister's Choice, page 69

Album, page 68

Album Optional, page 70

Best of All Set Blocks

Best Baskets, page 42

Bitty Baskets, page 42

Windblown Square Set Blocks

Windy Stars, page 37

For My Baby, page 37

About the Author

Sharyn didn't begin quilting until her son started school. He started kindergarten on a Monday and she started her first quilting class on a Wednesday. When she left the classroom that first day she was floating. Finally she had found the reason she had spent the previous twenty years plus sewing. She had tried most every sewing related craft prior to taking this class, plus she had sewn for herself and her family over the years.

Today Sharyn is just as passionate about quilting as she was when she started in 1978. She loves the teaching, lecturing, and writing almost as much as she does the actual making of quilts.

Persistence and stubbornness are two traits that have helped her master the challenges surrounding problem blocks. When confronted with a challenge it is her nature to meet it head on, and win. She will share with you some of her favorite problem solving techniques in this book, so that you too can feel successful.

She is a loving grandma, and is happily married to George. When she is not on the road teaching and lecturing, she lives in El Cajon, California.

Other Fine Books From C&T Publishing

An Amish Adventure: 2nd Edition, Roberta Horton

Anatomy of a Doll: The Fabric Sculptor's Handbook, Susanna Oroyan

Appliqué 12 Easy Ways! Charming Quilts, Giftable Projects & Timeless Techniques, Elly Sienkiewicz

Art & Inspirations: Ruth B. McDowell, Ruth B. McDowell

The Art of Silk Ribbon Embroidery, Judith Baker Montano

The Art of Classic Quiltmaking, Harriet Hargrave and Sharyn Craig

The Artful Ribbon, Candace Kling

Baltimore Beauties and Beyond (Volume I), Elly Sienkiewicz

The Best of Baltimore Beauties, Elly Sienkiewicz

Color From the Heart: Seven Great Ways to Make Quilts with Colors You Love, Gai Perry

Color Play: Easy Steps to Imaginative Color in Quilts, Joen Wolfrom

Crazy Quilt Handbook, Judith Montano

Crazy with Cotton, Diana Leone

Curves in Motion: Quilt Designs & Techniques, Judy B. Dales

Deidre Scherer: Work in Fabric & Thread, Deidre Scherer

Designing the Doll: From Concept to Construction, Susanna Oroyan

Diane Phalen Quilts: 10 Projects to Celebrate the Seasons, Diane Phalen

Easy Pieces: Creative Color Play with Two Simple Blocks, Margaret Miller

Elegant Stitches: An Illustrated Stitch Guide & Source Book of Inspiration, Judith Baker Montano

Everything Flowers: Quilts from the Garden, Jean and Valori Wells

Exploring Machine Trapunto: New Dimensions, Hari Walner

Fabric Shopping with Alex Anderson, Seven Projects to Help You: Make Successful Choices, Build Your Confidence, Add to Your Fabric Stash, Alex Anderson

Fancy Appliqué: 12 Lessons to Enhance Your Skills, Elly Sienkiewicz

Fantastic Fabric Folding: Innovative Quilting Projects, Rebecca Wat

Fantastic Figures: Ideas & Techniques Using the New Clays, Susanna Oroyan

Floral Stitches: An Illustrated Guide, Judith Baker Montano

Freddy's House: Brilliant Color in Quilts, Freddy Moran

Free Stuff for Crafty Kids on the Internet, Judy Heim and Gloria Hansen

Free Stuff for Gardeners on the Internet, Judy Heim and Gloria Hansen

Free Stuff for Quilters on the Internet, 2nd Ed. Judy Heim and Gloria Hansen

Free Stuff for Sewing Fanatics on the Internet, Judy Heim and Gloria Hansen

Free Stuff for Stitchers on the Internet, Judy Heim and Gloria Hansen

Free-Style Quilts: A "No Rules" Approach, Susan Carlson

Hand Quilting with Alex Anderson: Six Projects for Hand Quilters, Alex Anderson

Heirloom Machine Quilting, Third Edition, Harriet Hargrave

Impressionist Palette, Gai Perry

Impressionist Quilts, Gai Perry

Kaleidoscopes: Wonders of Wonder, Cozy Baker

Kaleidoscopes & Quilts, Paula Nadelstern

Make Any Block Any Size, Joen Wolfrom

Mastering Machine Appliqué, Harriet Hargrave

Mastering Quilt Marking: Marking Tools & Techniques, Choosing Stencils, Matching Borders & Corners, Pepper Cory

The New Sampler Quilt, Diana Leone

On the Surface: Thread Embellishment & Fabric Manipulation, Wendy Hill

Patchwork Persuasion: Fascinating Quilts from Traditional Designs, Joen Wolfrom

The Photo Transfer Handbook: Snap It, Print It, Stitch It!, Jean Ray Laury

Pieced Flowers, Ruth B. McDowell

Piecing: Expanding the Basics, Ruth B. McDowell

Quilt It for Kids: 11 Projects, Sports, Fantasy & Animal Themes, Quilts for Children of All Ages, Pam Bono

The Quilted Garden: Design & Make Nature-Inspired Quilts, Jane A. Sassaman

Quilting with the Muppets: The Jim Henson Company in Association with Sesame Workshop

Quilts, Quilts, and More Quilts! Diana McClun and Laura Nownes

Recollections, Judith Baker Montano

Rotary Cutting with Alex Anderson: Tips, Techniques, and Projects, Alex Anderson

Rx for Quilters: Stitcher-Friendly Advice for Every Body, Susan Delaney Mech, M.D.

Say It with Quilts: Diana McClun and Laura Nownes

Scrap Quilts: The Art of Making Do, Roberta Horton

Shadow Quilts: Easy to Design Multiple Image Quilts, Patricia Magaret and Donna Slusser

Simply Stars: Quilts that Sparkle, Alex Anderson

Six Color World: Color, Cloth, Quilts & Wearables, Yvonne Porcella

Soft-Edge Piecing, Jinny Beyer

Special Delivery Quilts, Patrick Lose

Start Quilting with Alex Anderson: Six Projects for First-Time Quilters, Alex Anderson

Stitch 'n Flip Quilts: 14 Fantastic Projects, Valori Wells

Stripes in Quilts, Mary Mashuta

Through the Garden Gate: Quilters and Their Gardens, Jean and Valori Wells

Travels with Peaky and Spike: Doreen Speckmann's Quilting Adventures, Doreen Speckmann

Wild Birds: Designs for Appliqué & Quilting, Carol Armstrong

Wildflowers: Designs for Appliqué & Quilting, Carol Armstrong

Willowood: Further Adventures in Buttonhole Stitch Appliqué, Jean Wells

For more information write for a free catalog:
C&T Publishing, Inc.
P.O. Box 1456
Lafayette, CA 94549
(800) 284-1114
e-mail: ctinfo@ctpub.com
website: www.ctpub.com

For quilting supplies:
Cotton Patch Mail Order
3405 Hall Lane, Dept. CTB
Lafayette, CA 94549
(800) 835-4418
(925) 283-7883
e-mail: quiltusa@yahoo.com
website: www.quiltusa.com

Index